LUTHERAN
VOICES

Connecting with God
in a Disconnected World

*A Guide for Spiritual
Growth and Renewal*

D1377995

Carolyn Coon Mowchan
& Damian Anthony Vraniak

Augsburg Fortress
Minneapolis

OTHER LUTHERAN VOICES TITLES

0-8066-4998-4 John McCullough Bade
Will I Sing Again? Listening for the Melody of Grace in the Silence of Illness and Loss

0-8066-4991-7 D. Michael Bennethum
Listen! God Is Calling! Luther Speaks of Vocation, Faith, and Work

0-8066-4992-5 Michael L. Cooper-White
On a Wing and a Prayer: Faithful Leadership in the 21st Century

0-8066-4995-X Barbara DeGrote-Sorensen & David Allen Sorensen
Let the Servant Church Arise!

0-8066-4999-2 Rochelle Melander & Harold Eppley
Our Lives Are Not Our Own: Saying "Yes" to God

0-8066-4596-2 Kelly A. Fryer
Reclaiming the "L" Word: Renewing the Church from Its Lutheran Core

0-8066-4989-5 Ann Hafften
Water from the Rock: Lutheran Voices from Palestine

0-8066-4990-9 Susan K. Hedahl
Who Do You Say That I Am? 21st Century Preaching

0-8066-4997-6 Mary E. Hinkle
Signs of Belonging: Luther's Marks of the Church and the Christian Life

0-8066-4994-1 Martin E. Marty
Speaking of Trust: Conversing with Luther about the Sermon on the Mount

0-8066-4993-3 Craig L. Nessan
Give Us This Day: A Lutheran Proposal for Ending World Hunger

Large-quantity purchases or custom editions of these books are available at a discount from the publisher. For more information, contact the sales department at Augsburg Fortress, Publishers, 1-800-328-4648, or write to: Sales Director, Augsburg Fortress, Publishers, P.O. Box 1209, Minneapolis, MN 55440-1209.

See www.lutheranvoices.com

Acknowledgments

I am grateful for the people God has put in my life, especially my grandmother, Martha Coon, who instilled in me not only the love of God, but the love of writing; my brother Jon Coon who has been writing coach, friend, and editor (and has published two books of his own!); and my sister, cheerleader, and life long friend, Janice. I am also grateful for my immediate family who gave me the time to withdraw and write, and for the many friends at Trinity who read it along the way and were honest enough to say "it's not ready" when it really wasn't! These connections are the greatest blessings in my life. I'm also grateful to Damian who initiated this project and was the soil that gave it a place to grow within me and flower on the paper. Our prayer is that it will bear "fruit" in the lives of others!

Carolyn

The love and healing power of Christ, first and foremost, seems to flow most directly through the love of my wife, Nancy, and then through participating in relationships with our children, Brook, Peter, and Stacey. My heart is deeply grateful for these relationships. In my helping efforts (including any writing I do), I try to pass on the love I received from my grandparents Alice and John, Joseph and Mary, and my parents, Kay and Ken. In this I am entirely inadequate in giving out the quality and measure of love I have received. A special thank you must be conveyed to retired Pastor Stan Klyve, who showed me a living model for maturing in faith I may never reach. For initiating choices that inexorably and painfully made me experience the fruits of betrayal and explore the requirements of forgiveness, I must acknowledge Anne Herring. Finally, I have greeted with enjoyment and pleasure a sequence of conversations over the past 15 years concerning my exploration and mapping of transformation within individuals, between partners, among families and small groups, as well as communities . . . J.R. Newborough, Jim Gustafson, David McKee, Tascha Boychuk, Tamilyn White, Bill Schmelzer and, now, in this project, Carolyn Mowchan . . . thank you for your companionable conversation and collaborative help. Yet, I must end where I begin, I am so grateful for your love, Nancy . . . thank you.

Damian

CONNECTING WITH GOD IN A DISCONNECTED WORLD
A Guide for Spiritual Growth and Renewal

Direct Scripture quotations are from New Revised Standard Version Bible, copyright © 1989 Division of Christian Education of the National Council of the Churches of Christ in the United States of America. Used by permission.

Editor: Andrea Lee Schieber

Cover design: Koechel Peterson and Associates, Inc., Minneapolis, MN
        www.koechelpeterson.com
Cover photo: Koechel Peterson and Associates, Inc.

ISBN 0-8066-4996-8

The paper used in this publication meets the minimum requirements of American National Standard for Information Sciences—Permanence of Paper for Printed Library Materials, ANSI Z329.48-1984.

Manufactured in the U.S.A.

07   06   05   04   03   1   2   3   4   5   6   7   8   9   10

Contents

Introduction and Invitation 6

Section 1: Contact
    1. The Biblical Story of Contact with God 15
    2. My Story: The Garbage Dump 23
    3. Your Story: Meeting God 29
    4. Overcoming Obstacles to Contact with God 45

Section 2: Connection
    5. Biblical Stories of Relationships with God 59
    6. My Story: The Ties that Bind 67
    7. Your Story: Comfort, Care, and Courage 76
    8. Overcoming Obstacles to Connection 86

Bibliography 96

Introduction and Invitation

Carolyn: The day after Easter, I made a quick trip to the church to pick up some books to read at home. In the parking lot of the otherwise deserted place was a single parked car. While I was getting out my keys, a man came running around the church from the back lot and asked if I was "in charge." Before I could answer, he asked why the church was all locked up. I explained that it was Easter Monday and we were taking a vacation day. His quick response was, "Ah Easter, the most depressing time of the year." I was too surprised to say much and he went on, "I mean there's so little evidence of Jesus' work and teaching in the world." The long and short of the story is that this man was not a practicing Christian, but he was a practicing musician. He wanted to get in the building for his violin lesson.

This book is for those who are interested in the Christian faith and who may or may not have left the church, but certainly feel "left out" and disconnected from God and from faith communities. Perhaps you come to worship infrequently, keep your spiritual questions and reservations to yourself, and find your faith increasingly irrelevant in everyday life. Or maybe you are just someone who wonders why some people talk about their faith in ways you have never experienced.

This book is the result of my own "search" and rescue.

Damian: Carolyn and I talked for more than a year about the strains and stresses, lights and shadows, of existence. What you see here is part of the process of our dialogue; a conversation between a male psychologist and a female pastor. It's a conversation designed to help you explore the lights and shadows of your spiritual journey and grow in your ability to trust our most gracious God.

Carolyn: The bottom line question is: What difference does God make in our daily lives? We believe that the Holy Spirit works in us daily to regenerate, renew, and help us to lead more whole and holy lives. Though we never expect that process to be perfect or complete in this lifetime, certainly the world ought to be able to distinguish between believers and unbelievers, Christians and non-Christians. What does it mean to say that we have "a relationship with God"? What can we learn in a world of disintegrating relationships of all kinds about the basic ingredients necessary to maintain relationships, including our relationship with God?

A journey of exploration

Carolyn: What's offered here is a journey of exploration, which would be best used with a small group of people who long to grow in faith and know God more intimately. Learning new practices, which eventually can become habitual, takes time and support. Working with this material alone, even if you are highly motivated, is likely to reduce it to the level of isolated experiences which may not help you toward the change and growth promised by disciplined faith practices. Each chapter contains exercises that may be too private for you to share completely with a group. But they will definitely help you search your soul for obstacles to trusting and being loved by God. Then there are questions for the group to discuss together.

If you meet weekly, then you might find and use other devotional material during the days in-between to supplement this study. If you meet monthly, then set goals for the time between meetings, like homework assignments that you can design together.

The book is divided into two sections, "Contact" and "Connection." Sometimes we have chance meetings with people—on the street, in a bus station, in a shopping line—that slide immediately out of our awareness. Other times we may talk for a few minutes and remember the other person's face or name, or the conversation for a long time, even hope that we might meet again. The difference is whether or not you have been fully present and giving attention to the other person when you met. Then you have made "Contact."

Until you meet someone regularly, you don't have a relationship. If you come to care deeply for a person in a relationship you begin to be shaped and formed by the time you spend together. A bond grows between the two of you. That's "connection." This little book is intended to help you experience "meeting God" in such a way that you want to meet God regularly. In fact, after awhile, with regularity your heart will be unsatisfied unless you spend quite a bit of time with God! How to care for that relationship is tending to your "connection."

From birth to death, the significant relationships in our lives shape and form us. Our earliest relationships imprint our very souls. It's no secret that parents and families have an enormous impact on our inner formation and development. Christians, as well as other faith traditions, also claim that God plays a parental role in our lives. The question then is, "How does God shape us?"

Personal transformation

Carolyn: "Life without Jesus," sang the preschool choir in the congregation I serve "is like a doughnut. There's a hole in the middle." The Christian tradition tells us that faith will make such a difference in our lives that we will no longer be on the lookout for the latest makeovers, diets, trendsetters, and personal bests. We can learn the secrets of being content in any and every situation. If you could bottle that, you wouldn't need Super Bowl ads to sell it. Is there anything that anyone wants more than contentment? Of course, what Christianity says about contentment and what Super Bowl ads say about it are quite different.

Christianity promises personal transformation, a process of becoming more like Christ himself. God promises us that faith will make such a difference in our everyday lives—in our basic wiring and response to life and to each other—that it's a new life. Our old selves, our old habits, our old knee-jerk reactions fall away as God replaces them with more faithful responses. That's the promise.

Whatever our Christian denomination, there's no ducking it: Christians are supposed to be different than their non-Christian neighbors. Even if these neighbors are good, moral people contributing to society, we the people of God know the promise of God: "See, everything has become new!" (2 Corinthians 5:17).

It's easy to give up on this promise. Many people have. Many people wouldn't pick up a book on spiritual maturity. Most of their reasons have to do with trust. I've been a Christian for as long as I can remember. I've been a pastor for a lot of years now as well. I've looked around at my parishioners and back at myself, and I often see a lot more brokenness than wholeness. Like many other pastors watching the numbers decline in mainline churches, I ask the question "What helps faith grow?" with increasing urgency. Like many other pastors looking at the difference in the lives of Christians and non-Christians, we wonder what leads people into more passionate faith.

Trusting God

Carolyn: There's more to this issue than we can measure with numbers, worship bands, and renewal efforts, or even with a list of individual faith practices for individuals, as helpful as they are. What's at stake for both congregations and individuals is learning to trust God. Do we trust that the biblical promises are true, or don't we? Can the peace of God replace the antacids we take for anxiety-caused stomach disturbances? Can the love of God make me less likely to yell at my children? Can the strength of God carry me through times of pain and suffering so that I need not live in fear of pain, loss, or death? Do we trust the biblical accounts about this? Do we trust the people who report similar fruits blossoming in their lives with God? Do we, can we, trust anything other than our own experiences?

I'm a baby boomer and so I have lived with the usual heavy load of mistrust, not only of God but most everybody else too. We are the generation who as teens and young adults declared that people over 40 were not trustworthy. We're now mostly over 40 and don't trust ourselves all that much either. So some of us have given up on any search for transformation and have settled in to grab the gusto, hope for the best, and medicate for better living. But some of us, restless for answers, have become "seekers."

I am deeply convinced that the heart of our difficulties not only with a relationship with God but with many of our significant relationships is that we live with a bumper-car mentality about contact with others. We are deeply mistrustful of the potential harm that may come to us if we are not driving defensively. Many of our contacts are mostly collisions and we have learned to bounce off each other to protect ourselves. The speed of our travel and the infrequency of our meetings are such that appreciating the gifts that God and others have to give us is nearly impossible.

A journey toward spiritual maturity

Carolyn: This book offers a map. It's the product of a dialogue between a psychologist with a deep love for God and a pastor with a deep passion for the renewal of the church. The map will help you look inward for obstacles to spiritual and emotional growth and will help you look around you for the traces of God in everyday, ordinary experiences.

When I first met Damian his concern for the disintegration of families quickly caught my attention. His work as a psychologist trying to help people grow into the ability to give and receive love, maintain committed relationships, and raise healthy children led him through years of developing models for individual, couple, and family well-being. I had been writing, preaching, and praying about why so many people have difficulty trusting God, following Jesus, and working cooperatively with the Holy Spirit's gifts. Our conversations quickly convinced us that these questions have many things in common.

Damian: I have been exploring transformation for several decades. My work has led me to think about transformation in layers. It seems to me that the clearest way to sort through vast amounts of information on this subject is to break it down like this: Work or development happens "within," then "between," and finally "among."

First, an individual can be well formed. All the "parts" that make up what we think of as a healthy and whole person may be reasonably well in place. We call this "integrity." When a person is well formed internally, or within themselves, they are then and only then ready to partner in intimate ways with others. For simplicity's sake let's call this first developmental layer the "within" work. Individual formation "within" is necessary before formation "between" two can go well.

When couples come to me for marriage therapy it's often the case that either husband or wife isn't well formed enough within to partner well. The focus of therapy then becomes individual remedial work to explore and help heal childhood deficits or traumas, for instance. There are essential building blocks to the skills intimacy requires. When too many of these parts are missing, healthy relationships between two people are not possible.

When individuals have continuous difficulty in the workplace, or cooperating in groups, like families or church communities, I often help them evaluate their partnering skills. Certain healthy processes of relating in partner relationships need to be in place before group functioning—"among"—goes well.

Obstacles to healthy development exist within each layer. These are the shades and shadows that we all know only too well. There are "little" shadows that are our own native flaws, faults, weaknesses, and maladaptive tendencies. There are "shades" that darken our relationships, one with another—tangled brambles of intertwining emotional and interpersonal underbrush that are confusingly painful. There are social terrors and nightmares that may overshadow the whole world as Nazism did in the 1930s and '40s and terrorism did after September 11. And of course, there is *the* Shadow—evil incarnate.

Carolyn: Now you may be asking, "What does this have to do with God?" Everything! A child needs a safe and consistent environment in order to learn an emotional stance of openness and trust toward the world. It's no secret that children who don't get what they need during their formative years have difficulty later in life. When parents live at a collision speed with a bumper-car mentality, children are often neglected emotionally.

It's our proposal that Christians who have not allowed themselves to be parented by God will not be developmentally prepared for partnering with Christ. Those who have not experienced intimacy with Christ will certainly not participate well in the body of Christ with passion or commitment. Finally then, this conversation is about spiritual formation, Christian maturity, discipleship, and the renewal of the church. It is about growing through spiritual infancy to adult commitment and caregiving for others.

Philip Yancey put it this way in his book *Reaching for the Invisible God:* "Just as we progress through the physical stages of child, adult, and parent, so do we also move through parallel stages in the spiritual life, though not in such a tidy sequence.

"Every person has three great 'cries from the heart,' says Jean Vanier, who founded the l'Arche homes for the profoundly disabled. First, we cry to be loved by a father and mother who can hold us in our weakness . . . . That longing may ultimately turn us to God, as children in need of a heavenly Father.

"Next, says Vanier, we feel an adult cry for a friend—someone with whom we can share our deepest secrets, whom we can trust without fear, whom we can love . . . .

"Finally, we have a cry to serve those weaker than ourselves. For many people, physical parenthood satisfies this need. Others—like Vanier the priest, like Jesus himself—seek out service to the poor, the lonely, the forgotten, the sick or disabled, in response to this cry from the heart" (Zondervan, 2001 Study Guide, page 133).

The task of "soulful infancy," then, is to learn to come into the presence of God for comfort and strength and to let that presence shape us internally, "within." Spiritual maturity is learning how to let

God help, learning to follow and not only to lead, learning to receive and not only to give. Maturity means trusting God's strength as our foundation, so that risking mature commitment is possible. This is not another self-help project; it is about God-help.

A word must also be said about the power that loves to separate us from God and from each other. Evil is greatly underestimated these days. God gives you the courage to travel with others, even though most of us would rather do it alone. There's that trust thing again. If you don't have the courage for that yet, then proceed with caution. It's hard for us to stay honest on our own. It's also hard to be honest with others. Often it is as hard to move into a consistent relationship with God as it is getting your camel through the scanner at the airport, much less a needle. However, God created faith communities because faith can't thrive without others.

Damian: Generally, as seekers we search for the comforting contact of warm closeness rather than cold distance. We seek the calming connection of kindness and caring rather than cruelty. We pursue the quiet generosity of thoughtful consideration and contribution rather than control, in order to influence the unjust, the unloving, and the unbelieving.

Carolyn: The process of spiritual growth begins by asking, How can we experience contact with God? How can that contact transform us within, shaping and growing our internal selves? That's the focus of Section 1.

You will need some quiet time, a Bible, a pencil, and whatever it is you do that lets you relax and really focus. What you'll find here are the basic ingredients for being truly present. Without this ability, genuine connection to God or anyone else isn't possible. We are often ships passing in the night. God slips right by us, unnoticed. And sadly, so do other people we love. This book is about making contact and building connections that give us the strength to live joyfully, well, and abundantly. It is about coming out of our self-protective darkness and isolation to risk trust in relationships.

For personal reflection

1. What motivated you to read this book?
2. What do you understand Christianity's basic beliefs and promises to be?
3. If you are already a practicing Christian, in what ways do you "practice" faith?
4. Have you experienced now or at any other time that God's promises are true?
5. Did you have trustworthy parents (that is, consistent, loving, and caring)? Did they provide what you needed in childhood?

Share any of the private reflection material you are comfortable sharing with one other person before gathering with the group.

For group reflection

1. How do you understand the impact of childhood experiences on adult life?
2. How does God "parent"?
3. Have you had trustworthy experiences with God? Tell about one you are comfortable sharing with the group.
4. How do you explain the enormous decline in church participation in America in recent decades?
5. What are you hoping for from this study?

1

The Biblical Story of Contact with God

I say to you:
still the body; pausing in place you rest
calm the heart; slowing the pulse, you recover
quiet the mind; emptying of purpose, you receive
until you no longer are other than what is in you to be

What has been created in you to be is what always has
been in you to become ...

   ↤ *Damian*

Carolyn: We are childlike creatures dependent upon a holy God, whether we know it or not. But how are we to deepen our awareness and experience of God?

Many people start by seeking a sense of childlike wonder and awe in nature. This is a good instinct. Somehow we know that returning to a childlike state of openness, trust, and wonder is necessary for our spiritual health. When we experience the tremendous power of nature, we are often reminded not only of the closeness of God but also the "otherness" of God. The untamable side of nature and its destructive forces remind us of our fragility and God's strength.

The work for us often is to unlearn the protective layering we have taken on in adulthood. When we learn to cover our hearts by keeping our emotional distance to prevent further hurt, or to reveal only the safest parts of ourselves, then we have learned to keep others out. When we cover our hearts this way, we also keep God out. When God comes nearby, we are often hiding in the bushes, like Adam and Eve, looking for fig leaves. We may seldom ask, "What does God have to say?" or "What does God have to give?"

Damian: In answering such questions about God three very good sources of help are available, three stories that provide excellent directions for us. While the second and third stories are yours and mine, the first, and perhaps best, source is the biblical story.

Carolyn: Christians are often taught more about the history of God's relationship with creation than the present creative activity of God. We often talk more about God's expectations for us than where to look for God's presence with us. How do we become more aware of the presence of God? If we understand ourselves as God's children, where do we look to see God's parental activity?

First, we invite you to pick up the Bible like you would a family album and let it tell you the stories of our ancestors. It will give you both language and a frame of reference for your own experiences of contact with God. The Bible is our "first reader," the book that teaches us God's "alphabet." God's Word captures the history of God's communication in the past and teaches us how to listen for God's Word in the present. The Bible gives us the tools to recognize God's activity.

Find a version of the Bible you like—many exist—and look up the passages identified in this book. Read quietly and prayerfully.

Creation: God's artistry and provision

Damian: The first thing we know about God is that the world was created, like a nursery for infant life, and we were lovingly placed in it. The first contact we have with God is definitely nonverbal. Look first at the elaborate preparations and provision God made for newborn life.

Carolyn: The creation story told in Genesis 1 tells us why we were created, not how. Read it to understand the reasons for the origin of human life and God's relationship to us as the Creator.

Let me tell the story another way: In the beginning God breathed. A mighty wind splashed the heavens with stars, swirling land and light into being. For six days God created: nothing happens all at once. Everything that is, is in process. The breath of God filled the rivers, raised the mountains, and put a tiny sparrow in the willow tree. Everything that has the breath of life came from God's first breath. Everything that has the pulse of life throbbed first in God's heart. Everything we see and touch that God created whispers of a God we neither see nor touch. *This is the Land.* Everything above and below the earth became the nursery for all living things and for us.

Walking upon the land, delighting in it, living from it, we explore, watching for the tracks of other life, other travelers. Who else lives here now? Who came before us? We learn what we are by learning our place in the world around us. We understand the present by looking to the past. Like Adam, we name what we see around us: moose, bear, eagle, snake. We learn the names of those who have gone before us. Their tracks are only visible in memory: Adam and Eve, Abraham and Isaac, Jacob and Esau, my grandmother, your grandfather. They all walked upon the land. Before blood was spilled and the first human bones were laid in the ground, there was this grand provision, a womb to bring forth life. *This is the Land.*

People have pondered this great mystery from the beginning of time. Something, someone, a power greater than any that we know set the process of life in motion and ordered it accordingly. Who, or what, or when? Just say that "I am, was, and will be" said Yahweh, the God whose name was so holy, so "other," so powerful, it could not be spoken from generation to generation. "I am: Look all around you and see my handiwork. I am: Fill your lungs and remember the first breath of life upon the planet. I am: Before you and after you. You are merely passing through my Garden. I am: See me in all that is. Because I am, you are."

This is the whisper of the wind echoing God's first breath of life. You can hear it if you walk carefully upon the land.

The psalmist put it this way: "The heavens are telling the glory of God; and the firmament proclaims his handiwork" (Psalm 19:1).

Damian: Direct contact with God's provision points us toward the provider. If we are paying attention, we begin to recognize that we also are part of creation. First, we recognize the nature of the world, the place that God has created and continues to create. This is the land. Then, we begin to recognize our own character and nature, also created by God.

The joined rhythm of the moon and the tides is also the pulsing rhythm of our heart's blood. The congruence is God's creation. What is outside is eternally wedded to what is inside—notice one and you can begin to see the nature of the other. This is love.

God's provision was the prelude announcing our arrival.

Carolyn: A certain receptivity is necessary, as with responding to transcendent art. Art that points beyond itself to something greater than human talent or skill is what we call "inspired." You can sense somehow the "breath" of a great Creator coming through the skills of the human artist. Look at beautiful cathedrals, listen to a cantata by Johann Sebastian Bach, and see if your mind doesn't go beyond the immediate to the infinite. Perhaps this is what Jesus meant when he said "eyes to see and ears to hear."

Responding to creation takes preparation and receptivity as well. If you want to see God's handiwork in the trees, that only God could make, you need to learn how to look beyond them to their Creator. You learn to see not only what God did in the past, but also what God continues to do. Evolution and adaptation are part of the wonderful story of God's continued creativity in the world.

The Word tells us that God continues to provide for all life upon the earth. Our hearts instinctively search out the provider. *Read Psalm 104:24-30.*

The Word tells us that the wonder and awe we feel toward the land points us toward God. *Read Psalm 8:1-4.*

Preparation for contact with God

Carolyn: Let's look at the stories of three people God spoke to, according to the biblical account: Elijah, Moses, and Samuel. We can learn from Elijah that the still small voice of God is comprehended or experienced most easily in silence. We can learn from Moses the value of turning aside and pausing. We can learn from Samuel that other people with more experience and knowledge about God are important resources for spiritual growth.

Damian: The Word tells us to wake, watch, and wait—that is, to pause and prepare for contact with God. More often than not, we are not ready to recognize God's presence. *Read Elijah's story in 1 Kings 19:9-18.*

Carolyn: The word of the Lord often came to the Old Testament prophets in isolated places, in the quiet. Elijah traveled forty days and forty nights to come to Mount Horeb, the mountain of God where he heard the still, small voice. He was prepared for contact with God. He called out to God and watched for God's presence. Notice that he was already serving God, acting obediently.

Moses was asked to turn aside and pause, to take off his shoes, when God spoke to him from the burning bush. If Moses hadn't paused to look more closely at the burning bush, he would have missed contact with God. He was instructed how to come into the presence of God. Notice that a simple physical activity of taking off his shoes—we might say a ritual action—helped Moses prepare to hear God speak. He also did what he was told, a simple act of obedience. *Read Exodus 3:1-6.*

While we might yearn for a burning-bush experience like Moses, we also want them instantly and on our time schedules. Fifteen minutes before lunch next Wednesday would be good, God. We don't wander in the wilderness often enough, stay in the quiet long enough, or step out of the daily earthquakes far enough to hear the still, small voice of God. When God does speak, we need the guidance of the biblical tradition and the community of believers to translate the message. We need other people to help validate and interpret our religious experiences. Many times we don't trust our encounters with God because we are afraid to share those stories with others. We are afraid that we just "dreamt them." Consider the story of Samuel.

Samuel's mother, Hannah, was torn apart in a bitter struggle. In her pain she turned to God. Her frustration about being childless led her to offer God a son, if only God would assist her. Samuel, the result of this promise, was dedicated to God and sent to the temple where priests raised him. Their lives revolved around worship and obedience to God. In this setting, Samuel learned how to prepare for God's contact and presence. An older man of faith, Eli, taught him how to understand God's communication. *Read Samuel 3:1-11.*

Notice that in all three stories, Elijah, Moses, and Samuel demonstrate willingness to be contacted by God and willingness to be servants. I have found that when people give up on prayer, it's because they keep asking God to serve them and God is not always willing to be our servant. But God is faithful to those who seek, ask, and knock (Luke 11:9-13) looking for opportunities to "let God be God." The journeys God asks us to take, like Samuel's, may be difficult. He was asked to deliver a message of destruction, knowing no doubt that kings often beheaded the messengers when they didn't like the message! God's work sometimes seems impossible. But God walks with, directs, strengthens, and empowers those who take up the mantle of God's work. *The Prayer of Jabez: Breaking through to the Blessed Life* by Bruce Wilkinson (Multnomah Publishers, Inc. 2000) is a book based on the idea that, when we pray asking God to use us in service, demonstrating our willingness to let God lead, God invariably answers those prayers. We can pray, "Speak Lord, for your servant is listening" or "Thy will, not mine be done."

Most of God's messages, most of the stories we read about God's contact in the Bible, have to do with God sending servants on a mission, often terribly difficult ones. Many if not most of God's servants were reluctant to take up the task, and therefore in the process they had to trust in God's strength and not their own. When I lived with my aunt who already had eight children, a lot of her communication with me had to do with chores that needed doing. In a world full of need, God has a lot of chores that need doing. If you are earnestly seeking the presence of God, you need to know that, chances are, you won't come away from the contact without a "honey do" list. But before you are sent, you will also be well loved. God is a specialist in comfort, consolation, healing, loving, encouraging, and also "tough love."

Contact with God then includes stepping aside, pausing, and inviting God to speak. The speech may be nonverbal. Communication comes in many forms and in many ways. But we are promised that those who seek God and those who respond when God seeks them out will begin to experience the presence and guidance of God. When we pray for wisdom and guidance and are willing to be parented, God is there.

For personal reflection

1. Have you had experiences of wonder, awe, and gratitude in the beauty of God's creation? Think carefully about those experiences. Try to remember how and what you felt.
2. Do you have places where you experience the holiness of God? Where are they?
3. Have you had experiences when God felt very close or present? Where were you and what happened?
4. How familiar and comfortable are you with the Bible? Do you trust it? For what?
5. What do you believe about God's current activity in the world?

Tell one other person something you are comfortable sharing from these private reflections.

For group reflection

You will need Bibles and a concordance, or Bible-by-topic reference book, or a computer with a Bible search program.

1. Make a list of two or three questions you'd like to ask God if you could. Spend some time with the group looking up key words in your questions in a Bible concordance or other resource. Read the passages. See what you can find out about your questions. For example: If God is good, what about all the suffering in the world? Key words to look up to find passages relating to this question: evil, suffering, God's goodness, mercy, compassion.

2. What do you know about God's parenting? See what you can find looking up "Your heavenly Father," "Creator, created," "God's children," "Child of God."

3. What does the Bible tell us about God contacting human beings? Look up: "And God said," "God spoke to," or "God appeared to." Watch for where the people were, how God communicated, how the people responded, and generally what the content of the message was.

4. With this information, what initial conclusions might you make about what to expect in your experiences of God's presence?

2

My Story: The Garbage Dump

Attend! To the reality of God's Creation, the Land,
Look and listen to the scenes and sounds.
God has made contact. Let this come into you.
Understand that God is. Experience what God does . . .

    🕊 *Damian*

Carolyn: If there is such a thing as an accident, I accidentally learned the power of prayer quite young. Like others who were inspired by the beauty of the Land, I found myself uprooted from suburban life and plopped down on a hillside in the country, where our television remained unplugged for more than a year. Like Elijah, I sought refuge by seeking God, while hiding out from life and pain. Like Moses, God got my attention while I was out doing regular chores alone in the countryside. I paused and turned aside. I found a place that I came to think of as "holy ground." Like Samuel, I had been prepared by wise and good teachers to recognize the presence of God and the answers to prayer. My first faith experiences were pretty simple; my faith childlike, if not childish.

Back to the Land

My first coherent memories of finding a window to heaven in the sanctuary of nature are rather vivid. Through a series of unfortunate circumstances, I was prepared quite young to commune with God. I had a broken heart, and I was lonely and isolated in new surroundings. My father had decided to move his girls out of the fast life of the city and back to the Land after my mother lost a battle to cancer and died very young. I found myself a "stranger in a strange land" at age 14. The friendliest things around were the rocks and the trees.

My first experience of country living didn't draw out sighs of appreciation and soulful peace, however. Far from it. For me, the valley where the house sat lay in the shadows of death, and the trees were only bars to the cage that marked my exile from everything safe and familiar.

So I learned to pray in the foothills of the Smoky Mountains on a ramshackle farm in Tennessee. My first heartfelt prayers were for deliverance, but not from exile, merely for safety as I passed through the barnyard on my way to the garbage dump. God has a way of entering life just as it is, inelegant and messy. A Black Angus bull lived in that barnyard. The ravine where we dumped our garbage was just beyond it. My lot each day was to cross over to the other side and deposit the day's accumulation. Perhaps many people begin to pray when they feel that they have garbage to dump out to God, but probably not literal garbage like this! For me at this young age, with relatively simple theology, the completion of this daily walk without harm was concrete proof for the existence of God. I learned to walk by faith.

With this chore, my ability to appreciate silence and solitude slowly began. Once I had slung my sack of garbage deep into the ravine, I would sit on a rock and dump my emotional garbage out to God. I remember identifying with Jesus in the Garden of Gethsemane, feeling there the weight of human garbage in his soul. I laid rocks on the ground in the shape of a cross and, like the prophets I learned about in Sunday school, I created a sort of makeshift "altar to the Lord" (Exodus 20:24-25). I found, however, that no matter how hard I tried, I couldn't control or manipulate what happened in that place. Something else was at work. Sooner or later the torrent of words gave way to silence. I ran out of words and felt empty. Then I was ready to receive.

If I looked south, I saw a steep hill, cleared to the top for a pasture for enormous Tennessee mules. To the east was a rocky trail leading up through streams and woods. If I turned my back on the barnyard everything else in view was inspiringly beautiful. God helped me turn away from the mud, danger, and barbed wire fences in my life and contemplate the beauty. The beauty and the silence were pregnant with the healing power of prayer.

As determined as I was to stay miserable and feel sorry for myself, I began to feel not only heard, but answered; not only answered but loved. Angels ministered to me there. They might have had a harder time making contact with me at the shopping mall. I would have been too distracted, too full of other things, to learn to pour out my heart and empty myself. I could only do that in solitude.

I learned to sing there too. Something in the experience of that place always moved me to song. Looking back I would say that in the silence I was filled with an overwhelming sense of being loved by God. I saw myself in God's eyes, if only for those brief interludes. God's love does call forth a response. I didn't only sing sad songs. In fact, even when I went there to cry I usually came back with as much sense of peace and joy as was possible under the circumstances. Since there were no critics in the woods, I got over the shocking sound of my own voice and learned to beller nearly as loudly as the nearby bull. The songs were my deepest response, my deepest prayers. God gave me the gift of music and I sang with all the schmaltz of Julie Andrews waltzing through meadows in *The Sound of Music*. The hills were alive for me, not only with music but also with God.

Beauty called forth beauty. Love called forth praise. Over time, when I wanted to escape the heartache of loneliness, I sought out the peace of God in solitude. Try as I might, I was never able to find that same comfort in the noisy words and busy place of worship, where I also searched for God. There I found language and learning and other seekers. But I didn't know how to be internally still in worship in the presence of other people. Initially I experienced God's presence most directly in the company of healthy trees, in solitude. That's where God got my attention first. I've never felt alone in the woods since, although I'm still rather afraid of Black Angus bulls.

Wrestling and resting in God's presence

While the woods hold great beauty, the ocean or other large bodies of water are also wonderful places to feel awe. I lived by Lake Superior for a time and found I couldn't go there without thinking about God. It always inspired awe. The ocean has its own built-in white noise, which is helpful for those who can't initially handle both quiet and solitude at the same time! It's pretty hard to feel independent, all-powerful, and self-sufficient when you stand at the edge of the ocean.

The first time we took our then small daughter, Sara, to the beach, she was in diapers. Always and still a spunky little thing, we delighted at her response. She sat throwing sand with both fists back at the waves, screaming at the top of her lungs. I was never sure if she was just furious that something could be so much bigger and louder than she was, and she was therefore not about to give up without a fight, or if she was merely delighted.

When I recall that picture now, I think of how many times people have stood in the presence of God wrestling against their smallness and protesting their vulnerability. Maybe that's why we don't turn aside and pause more often. Some people have a hard time feeling small.

I had no choice but to make regular trips to the garbage dump. I certainly wouldn't have established this discipline on my own. Neither did I thank my father for it at the time! But the regular discipline of looking beyond the daily garbage to a beautiful creation, spending time in quiet appreciating it, and learning to talk to God were the first steps in growing my childlike faith and healing my broken heart.

My story illustrates several principles about coming into the presence of God: First, I established a *regular place and time* to talk to God. The discipline of physically interrupting my day to travel to the dump wasn't my choice, but it imposed an opportunity for routine. Also, I was more needy than a lot of kids. My mother's death left me grieving and searching. We moved to a strange place. I had few friends at first. Therefore, my need and vulnerability prepared me *to ask God for help.* I had so many confused feelings and jumbled thoughts that I needed to talk in order to *calm my heart and quiet my mind.* I poured all of it out to God. When I was empty, God filled me with love and peace.

I can hear my skeptical confirmation students asking, "So did you hear voices, or what?" No, I didn't hear voices. The Spirit of God moves quietly in your heart and sometimes verbally in your thoughts. Somehow my own thoughts directed to God changed to God's thoughts spoken back to me. God's thoughts to me were direct address, typically things like "You are loved"; "I am with you"; "Don't be afraid."

"How do you know it's not your own wishful thinking?" you might ask. "God told me . . ." has always made me nervous when I've heard it from others. There's good reason to ask some questions. There are many things we might be hearing and not all of them are the Spirit of God. So we ask whether or not what we have heard is consistent with Scripture. That's a major question that needs to be answered. If the message from God is "I love you," that's a safe message you can trust. My faith community taught me, in song, that "Jesus loves me this I know, for the Bible tells me so." I was prepared both by tradition and Scripture to recognize religious experience. Until you trust and experience that, nothing else God might want to say to you will really matter.

Whether you simply feel loved, or your heart puts that into words, or God speaks in your thoughts is not important. The important thing is that you have an experience of being loved, restored, and strengthened by God. When that happens regularly, you begin to trust it. You begin to count on it. It changes you.

Next let's look at your story for places and times that God has told you, or tried to tell you, that you are loved. If your story is anything like mine you will soon recognize how many times you have given God the busy signal.

For personal reflection

1. Have you ever had an experience of pouring your heart out to God? What were the circumstances? What happened?

2. Have you ever tried to tell your life story from the perspective of faith? What's your faith story? Search for your earliest memories of religious thinking, feeling, or experience. See if you can put your experiences into some sort of chronological story.

3. If you have a negative history with God, what were the working assumptions you had at the time? For example: "Everything that happens is God's will and that was crummy!"

4. What has your history of prayer been?

5. How much religious education did you receive as a child? Was it helpful?

Before gathering in a larger group, share with one other person something from your private reflection that you are comfortable talking about.

For group reflection

1. What were you taught about God when you were a child?

2. Did you find your early religious education, if you had any, prepared you for adult faith?

3. Share some of your memories of feeling close to God.

4. Share some of your memories of feeling that God was far away or absent.

5. Have you ever received an answer to prayer?

3

Your Story: Meeting God

The antique clock in my living room faithfully chimes the hours.
Although it will have been chiming for several hours or days, I'm often
surprised that I haven't heard it.
It's like that with God.

  ≟ *Carolyn*

Damian: If you want to learn to come into God's presence, learning to regulate and focus your own "presence" is essential. Every person has physical, emotional, and intellectual energies. Until these energies are self-regulated so that we can be "present" and not distracted by our own inner life, it's very difficult to receive the gifts that God or anyone else might offer us. The level of these energies varies from person to person. Until we are able to be still, calm, and quiet, it's difficult even to reflect about our own faith stories.

Carolyn: When you search your experience for traces of God, do it with a companion or guide, as Samuel did with Eli. We need the support, accountability, and validation of other believers in order to discern and trust our spiritual experiences. "Faith, like chicken pox, is caught not taught," as a current adage goes. Undertake any new spiritual practice with the support of a community "where two or three are gathered" (Matthew 18:20)—or six or eight! Our spiritual growth involves learning that loving God means turning to the person standing next to you and recognizing your "neighbor."

What are your own positive and negative experiences of God? If your experiences of God's presence have never been shared with someone else, chances are they are secrets even you don't really trust. We invite you to reflect on your own history. This kind of reflection, like prayer, is contemplative and needs your complete focus.

Searching the past for your experiences of God may be easier than searching in the present. Like Moses, we often see the backside of God after God has passed by (Exodus 33:23). Searching our stories requires that we search our souls. Ask God to guide you.

Damian: The kingdom of the Creator, the kingdom of God, is before you. In order to perceive it, you must be awake. You must be *still, calm, and quiet,* emptying all the nothingness you have tried to fill yourself with. It is hard to be empty. At first, it may seem lonely and terribly frightening. But you are not alone; you are never alone. Slow down, pause, and stop.

Expectations and motivations

Carolyn: If you want to experience contact with God, send an invitation. Take a moment to think about your expectations and motivation. What can you expect from a relationship with God? Do you see religion more like a tranquilizer or a transforming power? If you understand the peace of God to be like a sedative that will make life less complicated, you will be greatly disappointed. Moses wandered around the wilderness for 40 years with a pretty unruly crowd of Israelites. Jesus sweated blood in the Garden of Gethsemane. It's a misconception to believe that people who pray more are removed from the struggle of everyday living and loving. A more accurate statement is that they gain strength and perspective to deal with these struggles. God transforms our responses to life and to each other, but God does not remove all suffering from human experience. Be clear about your expectations.

Start by telling God your motivation and desire. See the simple tool at the top of the next page. Be specific about making time and a place for God. Fill in the blanks.

You don't have to mail this letter, of course, but reading it aloud might be helpful to you. Sometimes people write prayers, sometimes they read them silently, and sometimes they speak them out loud. Prayer is simply communication. God answers prayer—but not on

Dear God,

When I think about my past, you have often seemed _____

_____

_____.

I would like _____. I desire this because

_____.

I am willing to give you _____ minutes of my day for the next

_____ day(s). I would like to meet you *(where)* _____

_____ *(when)* _____. Please

give me the ability to recognize your presence. I need new eyes to

see and new ears to hear. Please teach me how to receive your love.

*Signed,*_____

our time schedules, and the answer may be "no." We have been told, however, to seek and knock at God's door and those who seek the Spirit of God will find it (Luke 11: 9-13). So if you want to have contact with God, ask God to show up!

Now that you've set up a blind date, it's time to prepare for the meeting. For some of you this isn't at all a "blind date," but maybe you've been out of touch for awhile. Or maybe the last few times you've met with God, you've done all the talking. What do you already know about God? Do you have unfinished business with God? Are you angry, afraid, or anxious about this meeting? Take an inventory of your starting point.

I've only had one blind date. Those days are rather fuzzy now, but I remember that my friends set it up. I asked as many questions as I could to get some idea of the person I was going to meet. I trusted them, so I considered their information valuable. It's similar with faith. Where can you or do you get information? Use a piece of paper or two to complete the following exercise.

Resources

1. Whom do you trust who has taught you, or could teach you, about God?
2. What other resources do you find trustworthy for learning about faith and God?

Content

1. What do you know and believe about God at this point? Be honest and take as much space and time as you need. Use an extra piece of paper, if you need to.
2. What troubles you, if anything, about what you know?

Experience

1. When have you felt close to God? What was the situation? Describe it as clearly as you can.
2. When have you felt the farthest away from God? What was the situation? Describe it as clearly as you can.

My own understanding of how God works in the world is pretty simple. We are created with bodies that age and are prone to sickness and death. There is evil in the world and within ourselves that delights in anything that hurts or separates us from God and from each other. That's my definition of sin. I can't think of any person in the Bible who was delivered from all struggle and pain. Therefore, if I expect God to deliver me from all struggle and pain, my expectations are neither biblically informed nor realistic.

Many ideas floating around about God's power and intervention in the world are not scripturally sound. At the very least we can say that people in the Bible who served and loved God were not delivered from every affliction and a world full of chaos, evil, disease, and the natural aging process. My understanding is that God does not send us suffering or affliction, but allows evil because in order to destroy it God would have to withhold our free will. One of my dear friends once said, "Evil is like a parasite. You can't get rid of ticks without killing the dog and God won't kill the dog." Instead, God continues to inspire us to use our free will faithfully.

Much like earthly parents, God creates, nurtures, corrects, and guides, loves, forgives, encourages, comforts, transforms, and provides so that like the poet David we can say even in hard times "my cup overflows." And even in the valleys we can say, "I will fear no evil" (Psalm 23:4, 5). If you are going to see God's activity in the world, it's important to have some idea about what God does and doesn't do.

Preparing for prayer

Carolyn: Prayer is a time of two-way communication with God, a time of contact. The worshiping community I'm part of confesses each week that God can be experienced in prayer, the Sacraments and the Word, and the community of believers. This means if you want to experience the presence of God apart from worship, pray and read the Bible. Many resources in print describe the sort of receptive attitude for prayer we are examining here. There are perhaps more books in print on prayer than any other topic! See the resources listed on page 96, if you need more information. Here are some helps to get started.

Physically: Still the body

Slow and pause ... stay

Damian: Have you noticed that when you relax, if you do, at the end of the day you discover aches and pains or tension that you hadn't noticed as you plowed through the many demands of the day? The physical state of our bodies has a lot to do with our ability to comprehend God's presence. Consider this:

- Having too much physical energy, we move around too much; we are agitated or busy.
- Having too little physical energy, we are dull, tired, or exhausted.

You cannot pray or be contemplative, if you are on the move or asleep. We don't have to believe in the reality of evil, if we've been

The Interaction of Physical, Emotional, and Intellectual Energies

Aspects (shadows) of the Physical. Vraniak, 2000

Our task is to:	*Too Much Energy* creates	or	*Too Little Energy* creates
Still the body *(sit down, breathe slowly)*	agitation, too much movement	or	dullness (sleep, diet)
Calm the heart *(settle down, slow heart)*	excitement, too many moods	or	dampened (depressed feelings)
Quiet the mind *(focus, listen, sense)*	distraction, too much scatter	or	vacant, lax (not alert)

Awake *(the body)*	**Attend** *(with the heart)*	**Await** *(with the mind)*

Be Alert

tricked into constant motion. There's no leftover time or energy for God anyway!

Carolyn: I don't always know what drives me to keep working, or doing, or going. But I know I'm not alone in the tendency to overfill my time, leaving few pauses. To build trust and relationship takes regular contact. One shadow cast over American society is the pace we keep. It leaves little time and energy for relationships of any kind, even with our spouses and children.

I've heard many people say that when they don't have enough to do they "don't feel good." I suspect that what's behind the comment is that, when we slow down, our whole way of life is called into question—perhaps by the Holy Spirit. Rather than face that, we keep moving. Our "busy-ness" is a way of hiding in the bushes, and God is standing in the Garden calling us to "come out." We are often resistant because when we step into God's gaze we know that we are really naked. Our trinkets and trappings are, in God's eyes, only the emperor's new clothes and nothing of lasting value.

When people of various faith traditions prepare for prayer, they often begin with physical preparation. You might find the complexity of yoga, for instance, daunting and alien. But if you've ever been to a yoga class, you know that only when we have attended to our physical condition can we truly "sit still." When I work with children who have lots of energy, I always have some backup physical activities ready. I call them "wiggle tamers" for those times when they just can't focus on the task at hand.

When my kids were young and fell into that numb, and often crabby, state induced by too much sitting in front of a television screen, I would invite them to go outside and run around so that they could "come back to life." If you have ever gone to worship with a bad cold, tried to read a good book with a headache, or tried to sit in an uncomfortable chair for a long performance of a concert, you know your physical condition's power to distract your concentration.

It's becoming increasingly clear that too many people in America are sleep deprived or overweight. Yes, these are obstacles to spiritual as well as physical health. If the body is a temple of the Holy Spirit, we may have some foundational repair to do. We cannot be fully present to God or to other people if we haven't learned how physical tension, discomfort, sicknesses, and illnesses can be dealt with well. Our bodies become a burden rather than a blessing when we are not actively engaged in taking care of them. This is a spiritual issue.

The apostle Paul was able to deal with a "thorn in the flesh," some chronic physical pain, and still find great joy in loving and serving God. Some people with chronic pain are chronically focused and debilitated in spirit, others learn to live well despite physical discomfort. We may not be "cured," but we may be "healed" in spirit from the damages of physical hardship. The more common issue is one of simply being out of touch with what our bodies are telling us. When our bodies cry out for "more exercise, less food, more sleep," we often ignore these messages to our own peril. We can easily become numb to these physical messages and the impact they have on our overall well-being.

Damian: The first question to answer then is, How do you regulate physical energy? Do you have a high or low level of physical energy? Too much physical energy creates agitation and too much movement. Too little physical energy due to poor diet, too little exercise, or lack of sleep, among other things, causes dullness and numbness. And our bodies often contribute to emotional disturbance. Consider the behavior of a 14-year-old after a slumber party!

If you are going to sit beneath a tree and ponder your place in God's world, you need to be able to do so without falling asleep. You need to stop, then sit. But you may find when you do that, you have a few other things to attend to before you can ponder and pray.

Carolyn: When you are ready to pray, find a place that moves you to awe and humility, preferably outdoors—quiet and free from distractions. If it's not possible to find a quiet place outdoors (I live in northern Wisconsin where the winter temperature is often below 0 degrees Fahrenheit), then find a quiet corner free from clutter and distractions. Focus on God's creations, not your own. Focus on God's perspective and not your own. Physically stop and relax as best you can.

If you have too much physical energy to sit still for any length of time, you need physical preparation for prayer. A long brisk walk or stretching combined with deep breathing would be helpful.

Emotionally: Calm the heart

Smooth and soothe . . . settle

Damian: One of the reasons some of us stay busy is to avoid the feelings that surface when we aren't distracted by going, doing, medicating, or any other method of avoiding feeling. People recovering from drug addiction often say, "I just didn't want to feel." Like physical energy, everyone has a certain amount of emotional energy. Our task is to learn to regulate that energy and care for our emotional selves well. Like caring for our bodies, this takes awareness and discipline. The state of our bodies often impacts the state of our emotions. And what and how we think and use mental energy also impacts our feelings. However, the way to start is to move from the body to the emotions and then to the mind, not the other way around. Consider this:

- Having too much emotional energy, we are too excited and upset. We have too many moods.
- Having too little emotional energy, our feelings are dampened, down, depressed.

Carolyn: Doctors advise regular exercise as part of the treatment for depression as well as for stress, hormone imbalances, and other things that contribute to emotional disturbance. Exercise is part of the treatment for too many moods as well. This tells us something about physical and emotional symbiosis. I find if I'm really angry, cleaning my house with gusto is a great way to calm down and get a more balanced perspective, because it's a physical release of energy stirred up by powerful negative emotions.

Learning healthy ways to calm and soothe ourselves is an important part of learning self-regulation. In his book *Emotional Intelligence,* Daniel Goleman has some fascinating things to say about what emotional maturity and intelligence really are. He draws on the work of Yale psychologist Peter Salovey who categorized emotional intelligence into five domains: "(1) Knowing one's emotions . . . is the keystone of emotional intelligence . . . . (2) Managing emotions. Handling feelings so they are appropriate is an ability that builds on self-awareness . . . . (3) Motivating oneself . . . . Marshaling emotions in the service of a goal is essential for paying attention, for self-motivation and mastery, and for creativity. Emotional self-control—delaying gratification and stifling impulsiveness—underlies accomplishment of every sort. And being able to get into the 'flow' state enables outstanding performance of all kinds . . . . (4) Recognizing emotions in others. Empathy, another ability that builds on emotional self-awareness, is the fundamental 'people skill.' . . . (5) Handling relationships. The art of relationships is, in large part, skill in managing emotions in others. . . .

"Of course, people differ in their abilities in each of these domains; some of us may be quite adept at handling, say, our own anxiety, but relatively inept at soothing someone else's upsets. The underlying basis for our level of ability is, no doubt, neural, but . . . the brain is remarkably plastic, constantly learning. Lapses in emotional skills can be remedied: to a great extent each of these domains represents a body of habit and response that, with the right effort, can be improved on" (Bantam Books, 1995, pages 44-45).

What does this have to do with God, you may be asking? When you have strong emotions you haven't dealt with, trying to pray is like trying to hear a quiet whisper over an internal vacuum cleaner. You can't receive what God has to give unless you have some "space" for it. God can help deal with feelings. The first step is naming them, being honest about them, and then asking God to help you deal with whatever it is that's troubling you. It sounds easier than it really is. You may not be in the habit of naming or recognizing what you're feeling. God is probably better at this than you are, but the more clarity you have the better this process goes.

Are you angry and don't want to be? Ask God to take your anger. Are you afraid and don't want to be? Ask God to give you courage. Are you just emotionally turbulent and don't know why? Ask God to give you clarity. All of this is a way to simply offer up your feelings, releasing them into God's care, with the understanding that learning to trust God also means learning to trust that none of these feelings will cause you harm if you relax and let God help you manage them.

It is okay to be upset, angry, afraid, hurt, or sad. Read the psalms and you will see every human emotion that we know expressed to God there. Learning that as adults we are not at the mercy of our feelings, and that we can learn to regulate them, is a wonderful gift. Prayer can feel like strong loving arms wrapped around you until you rest in the comfort and protection of that shelter. Little children run for that kind of comfort when they are upset. Somehow we lose that natural and healthy instinct. Rather than run for comfort, we run from the awareness of the pain.

I recall what I thought was a remarkable way to handle the emotional outbursts and meltdown of a young child. On a camping trip with friends, one of their little ones began a full-blown screaming and crying fit over who-knows-what. Her mother simply and calmly wrapped her arms around her and let her cry. She didn't try to tell her not to feel. She didn't confuse her with a bunch of words. She didn't tell her it wasn't okay to express herself. She just held her. Eventually the little girl relaxed, put her head on her mother's shoulder, and fell asleep. The message? Strong feelings don't have to be scary, and after awhile they go away.

Whether you have too much emotional energy that needs to be released, or too little, the place to start is just describing for yourself and God how you are really feeling. It's simply a time to be short and to the point—name and claim what's going on in your heart. If you can't do that, ask God to hold you until your confusion lifts. The goal is to let God take care of your feelings for a while by wrapping you in love until your heart is calm. This is a time-out, not a quick fix. You can have all your "stuff" back later if you like. But for now just release it to God.

Here are some examples:
- Dear God, I'm afraid and weak. Hold me.
- Dear God, I'm angry and hurt, and I need you to give me a rest from these feelings. Hold them for me for a while.
- Dear God, I'm discouraged and lonely. Let me feel your love.
- Dear God, I'm ashamed to talk to you. I've made such a mess of things. Remove my shame and guilt. Help me trust your power of forgiveness.

If you are a person with lots of mental energy and lots of words, let me help you focus this process: It's not about explaining why you have your feelings. It's not about apologizing for your feelings or denying what you're feeling to put on a better face for God.

Mentally: Quiet the mind

Suspend and cease . . . surrender

Damian: Some people avoid their feelings by staying in their minds. Some people avoid their feelings by staying physically busy all the time and distracted. So they have a difficult time knowing what they are feeling and naming the feelings. You may have to stay put quite awhile to honestly name the state of your heart. Trust God with your honesty and try not to let yourself analyze or be afraid of the feelings. When you have acknowledged your starting place, then look at the beauty of your surroundings, breathe deeply, and begin to think, not about you, but about God.

Carolyn: You may find that quieting the mind is most difficult. Have you ever tried to herd chickens or excited preschool children? Sometimes quieting our thoughts is as frustrating as trying to get them into one spot. The more earnestly we try, the more feathers or children fly in all directions. I have discovered the relationship between body, emotions, and intellect can also be like this. Just when we are feeling physically relaxed and emotionally calm, the mind kicks in to overdrive. This business of stilling the body, calming the heart, and quieting the mind takes practice.

Damian: One of the difficulties is that we often go about it backwards. That is, it's common to try to use our minds to calm our hearts and still our bodies. If you think of this process in building block fashion, however, you can't strengthen the foundation from the top. When you try to think your way around emotional upset and physical tension or discomfort, it's never completely successful. Strong emotions often generate thoughts that wouldn't be there if it weren't for the emotions. Emotions are often generated or influenced by the conditions of our bodies. For example, there's little difference in the thought patterns of a truly exhausted person and a depressed person. Thinking, especially the wrong kind of thinking, can kick up more emotional turbulence and keep the boat rocking for a long time.

- Having too much mental energy, we are often distracted and scattered.
- Having too little mental energy, we are vague and vacant, lax.
- Learning to quiet the mind in order to enter a reflective, contemplative, receptive stance toward God and others is learning to genuinely focus and "listen" with our hearts and our minds. It is learning to be "present." It is much easier to do this if you begin by stilling the body and attending to your emotions. Then it's possible to let whatever thoughts occur run their course. Follow them back to their source and let them go.

Carolyn: If you are a person with a great deal of unexpressed feelings and thoughts, you may need to spend some time releasing what is built up inside you. You can pour your heart out to God in a variety of ways. My story about dumping my emotional garbage at the barnyard dump is an example of "emptying." You can do this verbally in prayer, by writing, if that helps you focus, or silently, if you don't have difficulty with this practice. Prayer journals are a wonderful way to get started with a discipline of both emptying and listening, then tracking how you think God is responding.

Damian: What do you know about your physical, emotional, and mental energy? Are you able to determine whether you have too little or too much? For the most part we don't stop to notice and map the interplay of our habits. What are some of your patterns? For example, do you swing from being too busy to then being too tired and exhausted?

Getting feedback from others is extremely valuable as you begin to pay attention to your own patterns. Your friends or family may have more accurate information than you do!

Moving toward a state of quiet and receptivity is not as easy as it sounds. Often when you stay put physically, feelings arise, and then when these settle, thoughts rush into their place. The order may vary for different individuals, but it is typical to cycle through each of these layers—stilling, calming, quieting, and then again, staying, settling, surrendering—until a sense of peace and presence is experienced.

Carolyn: In the silence let God love you. It's like sitting with a good friend when no words need to be spoken and yet the positive feeling is clear. It's like watching a child sleep when your heart overflows but no words need to be spoken, except perhaps a whispered "thank you."

Like your first exercise class, this experience won't do much unless you keep showing up. A relationship with God, like a relationship with anyone else, takes time. God will be there, will you?

Next, let's take a closer look at what gets in the way. It's time to peer into the shadows. That's the topic of chapter 4.

For personal reflection

Spend some time now praying. If you need to talk, talk. But when you are finished, turn your mind toward what God might want to say to you and "listen." It's best to start by simply experiencing God's love, without searching for content. You can do that by learning to be "still, calm, and quiet" in a sense of God's presence. People describe these experiences in various ways, but the common thread is a sense of being loved and cherished and an experience of "rest." Sorting out the difference between God's response, your own wishful or fearful thinking, or say, indigestion is not easy! The process is called "discernment." That means deciding what is from the Holy Spirit and what is not—destructive spirits can be at work in our prayers. I once worked as a playwright in the Louisiana prison system. I met a man there who told me God told him to kill his wife, so he did. Clearly that message wasn't from God! This is where faith communities and some basic Bible knowledge are most valuable.

The peace of God may begin to descend on you. If you have an experience of the presence of God, it might resemble one of the following feelings or messages:

- You're not in control and it feels good. (Rest in my love. 1 Kings 8:56; Psalm 16:7-9.)
- You're not alone and it feels good. (I will never forsake you. Deuteronomy 4:31.)
- You are loved and it feels good. (Nothing in life or death can separate you from my love. Romans 8:38-39.)
- You can re-enter your day with a little more peace and strength than you had before you stopped to pray. (His eye is on the sparrow. Matthew 10:29-31.)
- You want more. (My soul thirsts for you, O God. Psalm 42:2.)
- There are some things we need to talk about. (I will send you a counselor. Isaiah 9:6; 1 Thessalonians 4:7-12.)
- There are some things I'd like you to do in the world for my sake. (Tend my Garden, Genesis 2:15. Feed my sheep, John 21:15-17.)

If you can remember other times in your life when you've had experiences of the presence of God that fit with these simple criteria, jot down some notes about those times as best you can. Where were you? When was it? What were the circumstances?

If you don't have any experiences like this to draw on, is it because you haven't spent time in private prayer? Or are there deeper obstacles that need to be overcome?

Repeated experiences of being loved and attended to build our ability to trust that whenever we pause, empty, and quiet ourselves, we can receive the many gifts of God's love and the resulting strength drawn from that experience. Through regular positive experiences of contact we begin to trust God.

Share some of your private reflection with one other person before joining the larger group.

For group reflection

1. Look over the chart on page 34 and share with the group what you think your energy patterns are. Place yourself on these scales:
Physically

Low Energy _____ High Energy

Emotionally

Low Energy _____ High Energy

Intellectually

Low Energy _____ High Energy

2. What do you do to balance or regulate your energy?
3. What new practices might you try?
4. What do you have most difficulty with: stilling your body, calming your heart, or quieting your mind?
5. Share with the group your experiences of prayer, if you are comfortable doing so.

4

Overcoming Obstacles
to Contact with God

*God's specialty is making old things new, bringing life from death—
transformation. But first you have to show up at the recycling center.*

⟨⟩ Carolyn

Carolyn: When we try to experience contact with God and with
other people, things can go wrong.

Damian: These are the shadows, shades, and difficulties of everyday living. They may also be the influence of past or present evil in your life.

Carolyn: They are the ways we walk "in darkness," to use the language of the Bible. Chances are, your good and bad habits with the
people in your life will show up when you're trying the more difficult
task of relating to a nonhuman—God. One way to get at your relational habits with people is to ask, "When I'm sitting to talk with
one other person who wants to tell me something:"

- Am I physically able to relax, or would I prefer to remove myself
  so I fidget and squirm?
- Am I emotionally calm, or does intimate conversation stir up
  negative feelings?
- Do I interrupt because I'm not listening to the other person but
  instead wanting to share my thoughts?
- Can I really listen and consider what the other person has to
  say? (Does your mind wander because you really have too many
  thoughts to give your full attention to the person in front of you?
- Are you anxiously preparing your response before the person has
  finished speaking?)

If your pattern is that you have difficulty being truly "present" to another person, chances are you will have even more difficulty being "present" to God, or receiving what God has to give you. God created us to commune with each other and with our maker, but there are many things that get in the way of "communion."

For example, I have a teenage daughter who says "no" often before you get to the end of a sentence. I generally have to ask her to listen two or three times before she really hears what I'm trying to say. She's so full of all the things adolescents are full of— physical and hormonal changes, emotional extremes, and reining in the whirlwind of thoughts, peer pressures, and an emerging identity—that she has difficulty physically slowing down to hear the whole sentence, focusing on my words, and being calm enough to grasp their meaning.

Take a deep breath. Be honest. What does God need to heal so that you can take in more of the good from others and from God and leave behind more of the bad? If you are going to understand the stumbling blocks to your relationship with God and your relationship with others, you need a particular kind of self-awareness. Before you can begin to regulate your physical, emotional, and intellectual energies you need to recognize your current habits and potentially destructive patterns.

Self-examination, confession, reflection

Carolyn: I've never picked up a book on spiritual growth that didn't involve self-examination. Whether you stop at the end of the day and look for the moments when you felt God's guidance or moments when you blew it (perhaps asserting yourself in hurtful ways), spiritual growth absolutely demands the practice of confession and reflection. That practice takes time. It's called spiritual "discipline" because it also takes a commitment to regularity.

In *Reaching for the Invisible God* Philip Yancey writes, "Many Christians, diminished by misguided theology, need a healing emphasis on self-possession before they can think about self-sacrifice.

Wounded children must be healed before becoming capable parents" (Zondervan Publishers, page 244).

Further, wounded children must be healed, or at least learn healthy coping patterns for their wounds, before they can "grow up" emotionally and spiritually. We have to reach a certain level of "becoming" before we can trust "belonging"—attachment to other people or to God. Wounded children can be reparented by God and by the people of God. This is the inner formation work necessary before we can partner with Christ. Unless we can open ourselves to the gifts of God and other people, we can neither be parented by God nor partnered with others. Those who have lost the ability need to relearn how to trust.

Those who have closed themselves off to significant relational ties, or have neglected relationships in the pursuit of money or quick pleasures, need to relearn how to "be" with others. Sadly, we live in a world where people long for connection but we have forgotten how to talk or play or be with others without the benefits of alcohol or structured games or entertainment. Our conversational skills are rusty. When children go to play at their friends' houses these days, they often turn on the television or computer and sit in silence together. This doesn't grow relational skills in the long run.

Damian: Sometimes we have difficulty receiving love, God's love or anyone else's. Old hurts, perhaps from childhood, haunt us or cast shadows until we let the light of recognition and healing shine on them. Old wounds may have taught us to mistrust love.

We may use lots of ploys to avoid recognizing our deepest wounds. If our childhood or adult experience has taught us to shut out love, then we need remedial help opening ourselves up to the love that God and other people offer us. Sooner or later we have to trust and experience love, if we are going to be healed.

Carolyn: A popular T-shirt from many years ago read: "God didn't make no junk." I continue to meet people, however, who feel like "junk" deep down. God's specialty is making old things new, bringing life from death—transformation. But first you have to show up at the recycling center.

Let's say that you are frantically dogpaddling in the swamp of self-loathing or fear, trying to keep yourself afloat. Your body is telling you, "Boy, am I anxious." Your heart is telling you, "Fill the hole with something else." Your mind is saying, "Just don't think about it." The process of therapy is, simplistically, taking out the bad messages or habits to make room for the good. You may need professional help for this process. But there are some things you can try first.

Find the source of the hurt, name the message, and claim the wound. This takes some introspection and thoughtful memory work. Learn some new habits in response to your old wounds.

Damian: You can't make room for appreciation and gratitude if you are completely full of other things that have moved in and taken over. Before you can make room for love, you need to empty yourself of negative thoughts and emotions.

Carolyn: An annual Christmas ritual at our house is to clean out closets to make room for new Christmas clothes. Sometimes it's done more carefully than others! But you get the idea. Make room for God, find room in the inn, and find room within yourself for the goodness of God and others. You may need an old-fashioned house cleaning before this is possible. House cleaning takes getting in touch with your body, heart, and mind.

I don't know much about cars, but I do know that if the body is shot though the engine runs, the car is not going to travel well. If the engine doesn't run though the body is in good shape, then you're still not going anywhere. And if there isn't a semi-thoughtful person driving the car, it's not wise for that car to go anywhere. We often get dents and scratches, flat tires, and "heart" trouble that need repair before we can travel well alone or together. Proper alignment is a process I've heard mechanics talk about. In short, stilling the body, calming the heart, and quieting the mind are the alignments necessary for relationships. It is not an easy process, however.

People who try to fill their lives with things other than significant relationships continue to live faster and harder or numb themselves with excesses but seldom seem content, secure, or happy. The peace that only God gives is experienced not only in prayer but also in gatherings of people who love each other. We may look to screens to save us from loneliness, to solitude for safety, and to money for meaning. These are not new demons and idols, just the current incarnations of darkness in our world.

You can't love God or your neighbor unless you share daily life with God and your neighbors. If we avoid contact, making relationships shallow at best, nonexistent at worst, how exactly do we offer and receive love? Marriages collapse under the weight of our isolated habits because God created us to live in community. But somehow little children who grow up learning to entertain themselves and control their environment never develop the skills necessary to maintain relationships with God or anyone else.

Philip Yancey describes some of our relational difficulties: "Children of alcoholics learn that survival requires they don't talk, don't trust, and don't feel. They turn off parts of themselves that are needed for intimacy with others." He goes on to say, "Some people from dysfunctional backgrounds react in an opposite way. Out of a reservoir of unmet need, they cannot stop talking, they seek to trust those who are not trustworthy, and they experience an overflow of feelings they cannot control" (*Reaching for the Invisible God*, Zondervan, 2001, page 113).

Damian: For the most part, avoiding and distracting ourselves are common and ineffective ways of gaining temporary relief from negative physical, emotional, and intellectual pain. Long-term healing often comes from new practices that acknowledge the inseparable relationship between body, heart, and mind.

Coming out of the shadows

Damian: Stop and notice what your physical, emotional, and intellectual habits are. For example, a person who is flooded with feelings often begins to distract him- or herself by moving around an awful lot, and eventually ends in exhaustion either because of the inability to resolve the flooding feelings or the inability to stop moving because of them. And usually it's both. (Think of the teenager who can't get to sleep until late at night and then can't wake up until late morning.)

Another person may avoid overdoing and overwhelming feelings by spending great amounts of time thinking about things but rarely doing anything about them, and certainly not feeling anything (for example, the procrastinating partner or the "cold" acquaintance).

Do you spend too much of your time *fiddling, feeling, or figuring?* When things are too much or too little, do you *tinker,* are you *troubled,* or are you the perpetual *thinker?*

Over time, individuals may move from one little shadow to the next. For instance, unregulated mental energy (worrying and obsessing about something or someone) may lead to unregulated emotional energy (swinging through all sorts of negative feelings), which prompts physical activity (getting busy to keep it all at bay). It may take some time, but it's important to determine your pattern.

The inability to deal with and resolve physical and emotional injuries over long periods of time can lead to internal patterns of imbalance. But we can learn the process of naming, claiming, and releasing them thoughtfully. When we develop other patterns that only partially resolve these issues, we are only partially able to "get along." Partial solutions adopted to cope often have serious drawbacks. For example, sleeping in late can cause other problems. You may miss work that then needs to be made up. Past trauma, past internal habits of feeling and thinking, create an ongoing momentum through internal monologues that are very difficult to stop or even pause. For example, if you have been repeatedly abandoned or betrayed by people that you love, then in every relationship you may be consciously or unconsciously weighing the question, "Is it safe to be with this person or to trust this person?" Chances are if you are looking hard enough for reasons to run, you'll find them whether or not they are real.

Mapping your physical responses

Damian: Next, take out your pencil and fill in the blanks below.

If you were to identify one physical thing, one stimulus, that causes an immediate negative physical reaction (as my grandmother would say, "that gives you the willies"), what would be the stimulus?

_____

What would be your reaction? _____

_____

I recall a woman who would shut down completely if her husband quietly put his arms around her in bed when she wasn't looking. When she was young she had been sexually abused by cousins who sneaked up behind her in the house and then made her be quiet. I remember a young man who would not pet his wife's new kitten. When he was young he had had three cats that all died suddenly and unexpectedly.

Name two more of your triggers and your immediate, negative, physical reaction.

Stimulus _____ Reaction _____

Stimulus _____ Reaction _____

What are your relational patterns when you are tired, stressed, or ill? Do you fall into wanting others to rescue you, blaming others for your discomfort, feeling ashamed that you aren't always "up"? Do you feel guilty because you think Christians should always be joyful? Are you afraid when you feel physically out of control? Can you receive care from others without feeling belittled? Can you admit your need without feeling helpless or ashamed? Can you pay enough attention to your body to give it what it really needs?

All of these are thoughts and feelings stirred up by physical conditions. Take a moment to think about your patterns and make some notes here. Listen to your body. What does it say? _____

_____.

What are some things you do to care for your body, either to increase or decrease physical energy? Or discomfort? _____

_____

Mapping your emotional responses

Damian: Finding the origins of our feelings can be confusing. Negative feelings trigger negative thinking and may increase a downward spiral. Negative thinking is often not the origin of negative feelings. Trying to think your way out of feeling bad often just creates a loop that increases emotional tension. You may distract yourself, but you may also kick up the intensity of your feelings. Most people know the frustration of having a friend or partner, in an attempt to help you with emotions that feel out of control, say "That's not an appropriate feeling," or "Just don't think about it." People who are afraid of feeling anything intensely often try to shut down their feelings by running to their intellect.

Here are some helpful messages we can learn about our feelings:

- Emotions may be triggered by our physical condition and a physical interruption is likely to help.
- They don't need to control our behavior.
- We don't need to, and may not be able to, think our way out of them.
- They are transient if we learn to release them.
- Fear of our emotions increases their intensity.
- Trust in God can work wonders in negative emotional states.
- It's normal to feel powerful emotions in charged situations, but the emotions don't need to control our behavior.

Carolyn: Deep emotional sensitivity, or lots of emotional energy or range, is both a gift and a burden. Until I began to learn that my feelings were seldom permanent, didn't need to dictate my behavior, and that God could just carry them for a while when they were too heavy for me, I often felt at the mercy of turbulent thoughts and feelings. Early childhood experiences of prolonged grief without comfort hadn't given me the confidence that I could release and calm my own negative feelings. My fears of descending into deep grief and unconsumed sorrow kept me slightly unbalanced unless I had a friend, or surrogate parent, that I trusted to stand by if my turbulent feelings "swamped the boat." Deep injuries that leave emotional scars can sometimes lead us to unconsciously develop a constant practice of avoiding anything that might trigger those painful memories.

What helped? First, understanding my patterns and triggers. Then realizing how really trustworthy and present God was in those times of need. I was so busy dogpaddling I overlooked the life rafts. But they were always there. Learning that when I become fearful or sad or angry I can give those feelings to God, if they become too intense, has become a life-altering experience. My deepest experiences of God's love and strength now are often when I ask God to help me regulate my fear or anger, or to be calm in the face of intensity that's often frightening.

Damian: If you were to identify one thing that another person says or does that creates the most negative emotional response, what would it be?

Signal (trigger) _____

What is your typical response? _____

I know a woman whose mother was cold and unaffectionate. She never hugged her daughter. The younger woman later adopted children and pets and "unabandoned" any being that seemed left alone or apart from others. I know another person who struggles painfully when someone she cares about indicates they are physically leaving or might be leaving, or when they take emotional "leave" in the relationship. Her mother "left" her by dying when she was twelve.

Name two other typically negative signals and your responses:

Signal_____ Response _____

Signal_____ Response _____

Think about your emotional patterns. What do you do to regulate fear, anger, hurt, and anxiety? Do you avoid negative feelings? Do you fall in love with your pain and stay with it longer than you should? (Can you practice forgiveness?) What emotional scars from your past may still need healing? What triggers their power to "hurt" your relationships? Before you can release old habits you need to name and claim them. Before you can give them to God, you need to take a leap of faith and trust that God can help.

Mapping Your Intellectual Responses

Carolyn: When St. Paul tells us to think about what is true, just, and pure in life (Philippians 4:8), he's recommending intellectual habits. These are often habits we need to learn. Sometimes we have learned rather to focus on what makes us fearful, anxious, or unhappy. The premise of our society's all-pervasive advertising is that we can't possibly be happy unless we have more. The premise of our newscasts is that good news isn't news. The premise of a huge amount of television programming is that violence and darkness is entertaining. We learn to be greedy, pessimistic, and fearful. It's no wonder when we watch murder for entertainment that we are less inclined to trust strangers and less invested in friendships and other people.

It's also true that because we are currently overloaded with information, people often shut down their capacity for thinking through solutions and problems. They rely instead purely on feelings for making judgments. "Don't confuse me with the facts!" Many educators bemoan the fact that truth has become purely personal: "It's my truth and it doesn't matter if it's 'true' or not. You can have your own truth if you want, just don't bother me with it." Rational discourse becomes impossible when there's no acceptable standard of truth or authority. Our culture has been so completely sold on "If it feels good, do it" that, in my opinion, they have forgotten to ask "But is it right?"

How do we think about our "thinking" these days? How do we filter through our habits of mistrust, emotional bias, uneducated opinions, and negative mental patterns? If your parents taught you that conversation is primarily about venting your discomfort and objections to the world around you, how do you learn to focus on the positive, as St. Paul wrote in his letter to the Philippians? "Finally, beloved, whatever is true, whatever is honorable, whatever is just, whatever is pure, whatever is pleasing, whatever is commendable, if there is any excellence and if there is anything worthy of praise, think about these things" (4:8).

How much of our private thinking time is spent looking through old wounds and biases but hungers for a more positive lens? How do we learn to look at the world as God does? That is, how do we learn to believe that the world is worth saving, which is what God has done, and that we are worth loving? How do we learn to unlearn the messages that compete with God's truth? As people in Alcoholics Anonymous say, how do we get over "stinkin' thinkin'"?

Damian: Identify a word or symbol that creates the most negative repercussion in your thoughts.

What is it? _____

What are your typical thoughts? _____

_____

I know a man who begins to rant and rave immediately if you mention the word "welfare." He grew up in a good family and without a father, which meant he had to work hard and contribute income from an early age. I know another person who quickly and definitively becomes silent, or shuts down, when someone begins to pursue "touchy-feely," emotional stuff. His response to the suffering of his parents in World War II was quiet stoicism.

Name two other negative words, phrases, or thoughts that habitually are difficult to turn off:

Word (s) _____

What are your mental habits? Where does your mind go when you have time to reflect? _____

_____

Do you spend more time thinking negatively about your life, world, and friends, or are you able to focus on what is "pleasing" and "pure" (Philippians 4:8)?_____

_____

For personal reflection

Now take some time to think about your physical, emotional, and mental habits.

1. Are you able to determine your negative physical, emotional, or intellectual "triggers"? What are they?

2. What have been your typical responses to negative physical, emotional, or intellectual experiences? How do the people around you respond to you? For example:

- If you are sick do you complain too much? What is the response of those around you? What would you prefer?
- Does your physical discomfort trigger an emotional response? What do you do with it? How do the people around you respond?
- What happens to your thinking when you are experiencing physical and emotional distress?
  - What message does your body tell you right now about your life's balance (tense, tired, out of touch, anxious)?
  - What message are your emotions sending you (open or closed to others; fearful or trusting of life and living)?

3. How many of your private thoughts about yourself, life, and others are negative rather than focused on what is pleasing?

Ask God to help you change these patterns. Make notes about how that might happen and write or tell God now what you think you need. How do you think God might suggest these changes can occur? The answer to this question involves regularity and practice. That's the subject for the next section of this book, connection.

For group reflection

Share whatever you are comfortable sharing about your habits, triggers, and typical responses.

1. Talk with others about how they handle negative physical, emotional, and intellectual stimuli.
2. Ask if anyone has experienced healing or transformation of old wounds or experiences and how that happened.
3. Read the following passages and discuss them. What jumps out at you about joy, healing, and God's desires for us?

   Matthew 6:25-34 (anxiety)

   Philippians 4:4-9 (joy)

Proverbs 12:18-28 (In God there is life)
Jeremiah 30:17; 33:6-11 (God desires health and wholeness)
Hosea: 11:1-4 (God loves us like a parent)
Jeremiah 31:1-14 (Israel restored from mourning to joy.)
Philippians 4:4-7 (Let God know everything in prayer)
Psalm 30:11 (God turns mourning into dancing)
Psalm 40:1-10 (Those who make the Lord their trust)

4. Pray for each other's healing. Promise to pray for each other until the next meeting. If you are uncomfortable praying aloud, make notes to take home about the requests of each member and pray for each other privately. Ask anyone who is comfortable praying out loud to pray through the list, to model spontaneous, intercessory prayer. The content and not the way we speak the content is what counts. Trust God enough to know you can't mess up praying when your heart is in the right place!

5

Biblical Stories
of Relationships with God

I led them with cords of human kindness,
with bands of love.
I was to them like those
who lift infants to their cheeks.
I bent down to them and fed them.

❧ *Hosea 11:4*

Carolyn: If we meet once, coming into contact however briefly, we are acquaintances. If we meet several times we might say that we are "acquainted." If we meet regularly, and if these meetings are pleasurable so that we begin to seek each other out, make time for these meetings, and look forward to them, we might use the word "relationship." And when these relationships have a history and a promise of ongoing history we use the concept, if not the word, "connection." A bond forms between us, tying our histories together. These are the attachments that shape, bless, and grow our lives. I think of the old hymn "Blest be the tie that binds our hearts ... "

Unfortunately many things go wrong in these relationships that hold so much promise in the beginning. Attachments and connections are broken; they fade away from neglect, or we just outgrow them and move on. It may also be that we don't have the personal resources to maintain connections. The attachment of parent to child is a little less complicated than the attachments later in life, but still not without difficulties. Young children instinctively trust and rely on parents for their very survival. They have no protective mechanisms for filtering out what parents give them, and receive both love and hurt without question or defense. Children will seek out relationships with their parents unless there is something terribly wrong. Parents will seek relationships with their children, again, unless there is something terribly wrong. But when children grow they begin to pull away, as part of their natural growth process, but also because they may have learned that it isn't "safe" to stay close. These difficulties are only magnified in our relationship with God. The Bible tells us about human beings trying to maintain connection or relationship with their parental God.

We can see in biblical stories the power of divine connection and also the tragedy of those who disconnect themselves from God. We can also see how God helps reestablish connection, often initiating a process for forgiveness and healing. It seems in both the Old and New Testament accounts that if there is a constant pattern in our relationship with God it is connection, disconnection, and reconnection. If reconnection doesn't happen when we have strayed, it isn't that God doesn't invite. Rather, it is that the prodigals often don't return home. Sometimes those who turn their backs on God aren't miserable enough to rethink that choice. Sometimes those who turn their backs on God, though miserable, are afraid to risk "coming home."

Connection

Damian: Our attachment to God connects us to all other Life, which like the Land, directs our attention to the Source. The process of growth from infancy to adulthood, when it goes well, moves from a stage of complete connection and dependence, to independence and disconnection, and then to the ability to reconnect interdependently. Mature adults commit to others voluntarily, some becoming responsible parents of dependent children who start the cycle all over again.

Carolyn: God's design for humanity has always been one of community. It wasn't good for Adam to be alone (Genesis 2:18). God does not want to be alone either. We are created to live in relationship with God and with each other. God parents us. God's hands and feet take on human form when people are faith filled. So we notice that not only does the beauty and wonder of creation point us toward God in awe and gratitude, but so also do those people in our lives that are instruments of God's love. Loving relationships are a connection, a pipeline that allows us to receive God's transforming love. God ties a rope around our hearts. The rope that ties us to God entwines us with all other life. We become part of an inseparable web. This interconnecting process is illustrated in many biblical stories about ordinary people with extraordinary faith. None of them lived in isolation.

There's another wonderful thing about this web of human relationships: it's set in history. I wouldn't have enjoyed being a Jewish child in preliterate times having to memorize all the "begats" of biblical history. But I understand the reasoning: look how long God has been acting in the lives of people! God has been consistent. When we see history repeating over and over, we begin to trust it. That's how domesticated animals learn, for instance, that shaking a food dish means food is coming. That's also how God teaches us. But if we don't know how God has acted in history and we don't recognize where God has been active in our lives, then we don't have the strength of consistency that builds trust. We need regular contact with God to trust God. An occasional Bible camp experience won't do it for us. We need regular, reliable experiences of God's care. We need regular, reliable experiences with God's people. These are foundational for trust and relationships to grow.

The perfect plan in paradise

The Word tells us that God's intention for us is to live in relationships. *Read Genesis 2:4-25.*

God created men and women in God's image. I understand that to mean we have the power to create, the power to think and choose, and the ability to comprehend a God we cannot see. God gave us his blessing and put us in a nursery that was a perfect world. The daily routine in paradise included Adam and Eve walking and talking with God, caring for each other and for God's garden. We were created with the capacity for relationship, but we were also given the ability to hide from God and from each other. We have the ability to remove ourselves or to stay, to engage or to detach ourselves from God's care. It's called free will.

The transforming power of relationship

The Word tells us that those who rely on God will be transformed and grown, blest by their connection to God and able to be a blessing to others.

Read Genesis 17:1-7.

People cannot be shaped by God's love unless they allow themselves to trust, love, and serve God. God spoke to Abram. Abram heard a voice and fell to the ground. He didn't know who was making this contact and he was afraid. When he understood he was even more afraid. The One who was before creation, who breathed life into everything, who truly knew it all, the great "I AM" spoke to Abram. And drawing near to Abram, God offered many gifts, as many as all the stars in the heavens. God loved and God gave. And Abram learned to trust. In time, Abram allowed himself to become "attached" to God. He didn't pull away from the care that God offered.

Note the pattern of contact and connection that unfolds in Abram's story. God initiated the relationship. Abram responded with trust and obedience. He was willing to serve. Abram's trust in God shaped his very character and became the primary focus for the rest of his life. With that new life came a new name, for God was creating a new creature. God's contact, unbidden, and God's gifts, unsolicited, began a process of self-discovery. By seeing himself through the eyes of his Creator, Abram grew into that image. Not without some bumps along the way, but Abram became Abraham, servant and child of God, father of many nations.

God's sacred promise to Abraham was the ongoing blessing of connection. God promised many relationships, as many descendants as the stars in the sky, all enriched by their contact with God and held together by God's care. God also promised guidance and provision. God led Abraham on a rather complicated journey. And showed him where to "look" to see the true blessings of life. God's intention? If he blessed Abraham, Abraham would pass on those blessings in his connections to others.

Disconnection

Carolyn: Human rebellion from God seems to be part of our nature as the flip side of human freedom. The powers that encourage rebellion could be taken more seriously for there is indeed a snake lurking in every garden, in every heart. However you envision evil, one of its primary purposes is to separate us from God. The "shadow," evil incarnate, wins many battles and skirmishes, even if God is determined to win the final war. We are both saint and sinner, constantly in tension with our desire to serve and be served. We struggle with sin and separation until the day we die, but a life walked with God finally rests on the promise of God's mercy and grace, and God's faithfulness, not our own.

The fall

The Word tells us that in the beginning other agendas were at work in the Garden.

Read Genesis 3.

We learned to hide from God way back when we picked the first forbidden fruit. We've learned to hide from each other ever since we learned to cover ourselves with protective fig layers for fear of being too exposed. All too soon Adam and Eve pulled away from the hand that fed them by biting the forbidden apple. The story explains why we are often more disconnected than connected. They initiated "the fall" from a perfect state of connection to God.

Breaking the ties that bind

The Word tells us that, from the beginning, we have struggled with God's desire for us to live in loving relationships.

Read Genesis 4.

Cain initiated the first resistance to the gifts of other life, by closing off his heart from his brother, Abel. When Cain rejected Abel, he was rejecting God. God then disconnected from Cain and sent him East of Eden, where he would have to provide for himself. This was not understood to be a necessary part of adulthood and a transition toward healthy independence. It wasn't a transfer and a promotion. It was understood, rightly, to be a curse that would forever diminish his life. Loving God and each other grows our souls, anything less diminishes life itself. The voice of the dishonest serpent continues to whisper that we can be truly self-sufficient, as wise as God. That's the voice that urges us to disconnect from God and from each other.

Reconnecting

Carolyn: Time alone, if it is spent withdrawing from relationships, does not heal our wounds. The expression "time heals" isn't really true. Wounds can fester and grow with time. They can become "infected" without the cleansing power of forgiveness. God's love gives us the power of reconnecting when bonds are broken. God's love is the strength that makes healing possible. God can bring good from evil. Trusting God's love to be constant, we find the courage and strength to love again.

Pain transformed

The Word tells us that if we receive injury that God does not intend, by staying connected to God and others we will find healing.

Read Genesis 45.

Home, someone has quipped, is often where the hurt is. When the lesson we learn there is the necessity for self-protection, we learn to hide from others and perhaps also from God. Joseph, favorite son of Jacob and great-grandson of Abraham, experienced hurt and betrayal, separation and cruelty. What delivered him from the prison of his past was to remain open to the healing power of God. Generations after Abraham, his descendants were still experiencing the blessings of Abraham's relationship and covenant with God.

Our own stories of injury and hurt often leave us resisting God's leading. Like Joseph, many of us have received injury from the very lives that could most deeply bless us. God has the ability to take what was intended for harm and heal it, transforming our hurts as well the hurts we cause—so that we are able to give good to others instead of doing more harm. This transforming, healing power is experienced when we do not withdraw from contact with God and God's gifts given to us through others. Jesus said, "I am the vine, you are the branches . . . . Apart from me you can do nothing"(John 15:5).

The biblical stories show a repeating pattern of transformation in the lives of those whose contact with God was consistent enough to be called "relationship." Those who were open to God's bidding and wisdom were blessed with God's favor. Relationships include struggle but unless we divorce ourselves from God we continue under God's care. Israel's story is one of connection, disconnection, and God's efforts at bringing them back into relationship. People like Abraham, Isaac, Jacob, and Joseph had the strength to remain open to the other people in their lives because they had the strength, guidance, and forgiveness of God. They became a blessing and gift to the people around them. The human-God story is the never-ending story of those who trust and cooperate with God and those who don't. It is the story of connection, disconnection, and reconnection.

For personal reflection

1. Does your life include times when you felt closer to God or "connected"? What were your faith practices at that time? Were you attending church regularly, praying, involved in a

faith community? Do you also have times of feeling "disconnected" from God? How did you "reconnect" if you have?

2. Have you ever drawn on strength from God during times of stress? Think about those experiences. How was God "present" to you? If you were not able to comprehend God's presence, what were the circumstances?

3. Have you ever had difficulty practicing forgiveness in your relationships with others? Have you ever found peace and healing, as Joseph did, through practicing forgiveness? Think about how God might have been working behind the scenes in your life in these situations.

For group reflection

You may need some Bible helps to do this activity well. You can usually find these in a church library or ask your pastor for resources.

1. Look up any of the central characters of the Old Testament and trace their story with God.

2. How many stories do you know from the Bible that include the pattern connection, disconnection, reconnection with God? Spend some time looking for the causes of disconnection, the consequences, and the ways that reconnection happened.

3. What do these stories tell you about God?

4. What do these stories tell you about God's intention for your relationships with others?

5. Spend some time sharing the results of your research together. What patterns can you find? What stories help us recognize our own patterns? Have people changed much today? Has God?

6

My Story: The Ties That Bind

Connected
The cord that tied us to our mothers
        before we could see or speak,
is a cord that gives the gift of life.
In those prebirth days before coming into the world
        attachment was necessary for life.
Even when the cord is no longer needed for nourishment
        · *a baby quickly grows another kind of attachment.*
Mother is life. Mother is touch. Mother is safe.
Reliable contact teaches little ones a primitive trust,
        a heartfelt, but invisible rope, the heart's cord,
the connection to life, strength for the early growth.
The baby will not thrive or even survive without it.
It is still attachment that gives us growth and life.

⟨⁂⟩ *Carolyn*

Carolyn: Many believers aren't able to put aside their fear of being essentially alone in a world without God because they are not able to connect their experiences of God into a pattern of positive memories.

When we are not looking for traces of God, it's easy to greatly undervalue the gifts of the present and the hand that has provided them. As imperfect as they always are, the family and friends who are capable of passing on God's love and care to us are the most tangible vessels of God's love and grace that we will ever know. The deepest pains we experience are to be left behind when those loved ones die or to be betrayed by the very people who could most profoundly bless us. No matter how we try to isolate ourselves from the vulnerability of the need to love and be loved, it doesn't work. Even God isn't satisfied to be alone. Yet we often live oblivious to the treasures close at hand. While kneeling at our bedsides begging God to ease the loneliness of our hearts, we refuse to answer the telephone where we might receive the answer to our prayers.

Looking back through my own history for the tracks of God, what comes to mind first are significant life events of joy and sorrow. Looking for God, I find the faces of those who shared those experiences with me. Sometimes they were people I barely knew. Sometimes they were lifelong friends. God's angels take many shapes, and they are seldom recognized, especially if they come disguised as family. The trouble I have recognizing the presence of God in family members is that they come packaged with a lot of trappings that don't look much like what I know of God. I don't expect God to speak through a Moses who stutters or come to earth in a ramshackle barn, but God did. Sometimes all I can see is the clutter and not the Spirit of God. It takes a quiet heart to see clearly, stay open, and discard what is not from God.

The people who have influenced or altered the course of my life or the sculpting of my soul are those I have had regular contact with over a longer course of time. Some have taught me the strength of faith and commitment. Some have taught me the fear of abandonment and betrayal. Some have been connecting links to healing from the wounds of disconnection. I suspect most people can look over their past relationships and see similar patterns.

Children learn to look at the world through their parents' eyes. They learn to look at themselves too. We learn not only how to name things when they teach us our first words; we also learn how to understand what we name. "This is fire. It's hot. Don't touch." "This is love. This is not." In an imperfect world, some of what we learn will have to be unlearned later on, because both parents and children are imperfect.

We learn many of our emotional and intellectual habits in childhood. Parents give children a lot of messages about what to do with their energies. Children can learn habits of anxiety, trust, fear, optimism, pessimism, helplessness, or hope from their parents. They also learn habits of faith or lack of them. Young children can learn to delight in their surroundings or to focus on what they do not or cannot have. This isn't entirely the fault of advertising, however, because Adam and Eve had the same difficulties! In a television documentary I watched, the program reported that children of concentration camp victims often displayed more anxiousness than the survivors themselves. Emotional habits are often learned responses. It could be that the sins of the fathers are indeed passed down through the generations.

Go-betweens

I was fortunate to have a mother and a grandmother who fixed my eyes toward heaven. When I was fairly young, old enough to remember now, but young enough to not quite understand then, watching my grandmother eat lunch profoundly shaped my understanding of God. She was a small Scotch Presbyterian who moved in with my family after retiring from teaching Latin and Greek at a small church college in South Dakota. Her retirement immediately meant taking primary responsibility for raising three children and running a household so that my mother, also a professional woman, could work full time.

It was my grandmother, Martha Coon, who taught me about a relationship with God. She liked to take her meals alone, in the little apartment attached to our house where she had separate space and living quarters. Entrance to my grandmother's part of the house was by invitation only. So I considered it a treat to be invited to watch my grandmother eat hard-boiled eggs and read her Bible. Her lunchtime was the time she set aside to spend with God. I don't remember how often I was invited or what I had for lunch. But I do remember watching her while she read her Bible in Greek, with little comment. Years later when I entered the seminary, she sent me that same little Greek New Testament. It was a very precious gift.

There weren't a lot of words from her about her faith. But the general balance, peace, and dignity of her life spoke volumes. In everyone's eyes, including my rather skeptical father's, she was the family treasure. She had an enormous sense of wisdom and integrity that made you want to sit up straight in her presence and pay attention. She was the anchor in my family's all-too-often storm and stress. She had the marvelous ability to be curious and interested in everything around her. When she was ninety years old she read the then popular book *I'm OK, You're OK* by Thomas Anthony Harris, learned to play the organ, and took a correspondence course to improve her writing skills. She liked to remark that if she didn't get her homework in on time her instructor would think she died. She was a model of the strength it took to stay open to all of life, for all of her life.

Home is also where our hearts are tended, mended, and grown. It is where our foundations are formed. My grandmother's life modeled for me the strength and transforming power of a relationship with God. Her father was an alcoholic, her mother died young in the pioneer's battle to homestead that claimed so many lives. She was led, I think by God, to be a pioneer of women's roles and took that journey with quiet dignity. Her wayward son often broke her heart, but she persisted with care and love. She exuded respect for life and God, and the only explanation I could come to, even as a young child, was her open dependence on God. Like a fire, it drew me closer and captured my attention. I wanted to see life through her eyes, which meant learning to seek God in everyday life. She taught me how to trust my own experiences of God's care and connection. I had to learn to value what she valued, which meant learning to look at others through God's eyes. That has been a slow, lifelong journey. Gram and others like her have pointed out the way.

Disconnected

When people live in fear of each other, they have little strength to draw on for healing and growth. They are turned in upon themselves. When people don't trust God, they have little to draw on for hope and strength when their own is depleted. In order to trust God's providence and power, people need the ability to recognize God's presence in their world and in their lives. Too often we discount our own experiences of contact with God. We discount the gifts of the people around us and deflect the good things that they may try to give us. How quickly we forget praise and how long we remember sharp criticism! Expecting pain, we distrust love. We may believe in God, but we often don't trust God to act on our behalf. We fear that we are alone.

Most of the suffering I experienced earlier in my life was greatly increased by the fear that it could get worse and that I'd have to handle it alone. I've noticed that you usually get what you expect. Essentially orphaned at age twelve, I closed down as a protective stance against pain. But shutting out pain also means shutting out love. Unfortunately what's appropriate for survival at one time in our lives may be completely inappropriate when the situations change. Paraphrasing one of my favorite quotations from Alfred North Whitehead, a philosopher: The trick of evil is to urge a good thing at the wrong time.

Remedial connecting

The task for me has been to let the love of God seep into my living so that my own heart would be more capable of giving and receiving love. I quickly discovered the difficulty was learning to still, calm, and quiet myself so that I could empty enough and open enough to receive.

Co-authoring this book has meant not only to write but to live the experience. I thought myself a rather quiet and contemplative person when Damian and I started this project. I quickly discovered that I had too much pent up physical energy to really be still. I had way too many emotional wounds to calm the fears of my heart. And I am intensely thoughtful, so to quiet my mind is a formidable task. It has taken a year of rather constant coaching from

Damian, silent but powerful prayer support from the intercessors in my life, combined with the discipline of continually trying to voice the principles and the process.

How can I capture for you the real heart of what has been powerfully transforming for me? It's one thing to name what needs to happen. It's something else again to realize how many obstacles there are, and how slowly this transformation really occurs.

I thought myself well grounded in a heartfelt relationship with God. I'm a pastor, after all, and deeply passionate about my work. What I discovered, however, is that although I give care, concern, and love rather easily to others, I deflect most of what others would give to me. My defenses didn't let God's love or human love grow my heart or stabilize my soul. It may be more blessed to give than to receive, but if you can't trust the giver, any giver, there's no place to find rest and renewal. When I met Damian, my emotional well had run dry and I was "running on empty," as the saying goes. Like a good many people I know, my schedule seemed frantic, my stress level high, my self-care pretty minimal and my capacity for being still, calm, and quiet was a joke. No one close to me, however, was laughing. My husband has often described me as one who doesn't know when to stop working. I have pushed the limits of my energy so often that I've frequently lived quite close to the edge of collapse. Like most workaholics I have expected other people to enable this behavior because of the benefit—the good work I produce. This rationale eventually wears thin with family and friends. The result is often bitterness and resentment about the relational things that don't happen when constant busy-ness is the norm.

My relationship with Damian began with the simple question: "Can you help me learn how not to work so hard?" The reason for the pace I kept was, in part, trying to outrun the feelings and thoughts that caught up with me when I slowed down. I used work as a distraction. I needed to learn how to still, calm, and quiet, so that

I could heal. Healing takes place within relationships of trust. Without trust, love's power can't be received. So how do we rebuild the capacity for trust? Those of us who have hit a few too many bumps in the road have deflated the ability to sit back and enjoy the ride unless we're driving, albeit white-knuckled, down the road.

The idea that God is my copilot is far from comforting to me. We may say that God holds us in God's hands but it's my experience that every now and then God claps. I am completely willing to serve God, but I have been unable to let "perfect love cast out fear." In other words, I haven't been able to trust God.

My own journey, then, has been coming to terms with suffering. Rather than receiving love and support from others or God during times of grief, loss, or pain, I have tended to withdraw into deep and lonely emotional isolation and fear. All the while, during these times, feeling that I was unfaithful for not being able to find peace and serenity in my relationship with God. The wear and tear of this tension has often left me in despair.

Opening to receive and to heal began for me with one person being incredibly patient and trustworthy, and of course very skilled. The experience was like the chipmunk I hand-tamed last summer by holding my hand full of sunflower seeds and remaining calm and still many, many, times. Damian did the same for me. Through regular contact that was safe, reliable, and healing, I began to trust "connection." When that happened I became able to take in what I needed for healing.

I was able to name and claim the feelings that so often overwhelmed and confused me earlier in life. I was able to come out of the shadow of past hurts and learn new responses to the physical, emotional, and intellectual "triggers" I had adopted along the way. This is a subtle and slow process. For example, I used to be terribly anxious when my children or my husband left home for any length of time to go on trips without me. Realizing that this was the fear of abandonment and loss triggered from my childhood has let me recognize the feeling, pray for their safety, and rest in God's love. This was particularly important recently when my oldest daughter began college. She sends me e-mail notes "Mom, are you okay?" much more often than I send the same notes to her! With help I have learned to stop running and to be open to learning new things, to calm my emotions by releasing my feelings, and to learn new thinking habits and self-regulation skills. Once that happened I could really let God's love in. This set off a positive chain reaction in all of my relationships.

This naming and claiming of feelings was an intense experience. It almost always pointed beyond Damian's skill to God's love. People who need the kind of healing I needed probably need more than this book can offer. But if the body of Christ can function to incarnate love and care for each other, small groups of committed people can be the support for this kind of journey.

The emptying process is more complicated than I ever imagined but very necessary. Those old archaic wounds from the past are deeply buried and embedded into our coping patterns. They don't just pop up in the 30 seconds of time allowed for confession in most worship services! And our past hurts are usually accompanied by powerful emotions that may not feel "safe." There are reasons that we avoid feeling pain. One is the fear that we can't survive it. I'm struck by how often people refer to crying as "losing it." And yet crying is a natural part of the healing process.

We need the support of others in our attempts at better care for our bodies and better habits of heart and mind. Be advised: Do not try to do this alone! The gifts of God do flow to us through others. We must learn to open and receive them. Seek and you will find.

Once I made room for God, I found this quote from my friend JoAnn Nesser's book, *Journey into Reality: Through Prayer and God-Centeredness (Living Waters, 1998),* to be very true:

We need to seek God's face and come into God's presence with the complete abandon a child would have: totally unaware of our naked-ness, focused outward, focused on God instead of on self. We need to come unashamedly into God's presence. How can we do this? How can we get to the place where we can come in? One way is by medi-tating on scripture, particularly on the parts of scripture which say things like, 'Because you are precious in my sight . . . Let the words soak in: God says this with many different words . . . Pray verses like these, meditate on them, let the words soak in to replace all the lies laid up inside you over the years. (page 36)

For personal reflection

1. As a child, what lessons did you learn that help you trust relationships?
2 As a child, what lessons did you learn that still create prob-lems in your relationships?
3. Who or what has been helpful along the way for healing, forgiveness, and new emotional and spiritual growth?
4. When you listen for God's messages to you, what sorts of things do you hear?

For group reflection

1. As much you are comfortable in doing so, tell about important life lessons you've learned in your significant life relationships.
2. What experiences do you carry with you that give you strength and hope for the future?
3. What experiences do you carry with you that get in the way of relationships with others and with God?

7

Your Story: Comfort, Care, and Courage

Slow and pause, still, calm, and quiet
> *Then*
> *Regularly, open and receive the gifts of God.*
> *Many of them come through others.*
> *Then*
Trust God's providential contact to be eternal.

    ✒ *Damian*

Damian: What we most need and value in significant relationships makes up a pretty simple list. When we receive comfort from others we learn to value gentleness and patience. When we receive care from others we learn to value warmth and kindness and the importance of tolerance. When people treat us considerately we learn the shaping influence of being given respect generously. We experience the stabilizing power of being welcomed, valued, and respected.

Early in our lives, however, we may have been given other things. Playground lessons often teach fear instead of love. Childhood experiences that remain unhealed can impair our ability to trust anyone or God. If we have received too much hurt, we may close down altogether. Rather than learning to sort the pieces, we lose our ability to receive anything from others. We learn to close off or strike out and protect ourselves from danger and harm, unfortunately filtering out the good with the bad. The courage to suffer pain for the sake of love is the message of sacrificial love and the cross. However, this is often misinterpreted as an encouragement to endure abuse. That's not the point. But if we never risk love for those who do not return our love (or even risk loving our enemies), are we any different than unbelievers? Jesus said, "Love your enemies and pray for those who persecute you" (Matthew 5:20). Having a broken heart is also breaking a heart open. Praying for those who have hurt you is a way to release the power of the hurt and open the heart to forgiveness. This is necessary for our own well-being. But it doesn't mean that you place yourself in harm's way or become a doormat to abuse!

Before you can experience and receive the gifts that other people offer you in your relationships, you need to know how to value and appreciate them. But if we are fearful, we often deflect and close ourselves off from receiving these kinds of gifts. Likewise, before we can incorporate God's love into our living as a strength and resource to draw from, we need to be open enough to receive it. In so doing, we will be filled.

Aspects of the most significant relationships in our lives shape our souls. There are four basic characteristics of living in relationship that are crucial to incorporating God's love into our center of our living: *gentleness, kindness, respect* and *honor*.

To be *gentle* is not to grasp or grab or crush. To be gentle is to touch—softly—as a mother touches her newborn child. To be *kind* is not to withhold or to be coldly distant. To be kind is to share warm feelings—with the heart it is to smile warmly in the harshest of atmospheres, to find laughter in the most serious moments, to care when caring seems to be difficult. To be *respectful* is to have sensitive thoughts of others—to understand clearly and cleanly what is offered from others. It is to know what is the best of the communications and gifts offered by others. To *honor* is to voice what is in one's body and heart and mind—to express simply and clearly and directly what is most beautiful and meaningful in our living.

In my childhood I learned to track and to hunt and to be an exceptional athlete, that is, I learned the value of being physically fit. Oh, I pounded the earth in my stalking and vital power! Then, more recently, I learned how to balance my self and physically fit my self to mother earth, to move and touch her body gently.

In my youth, I was taught how to deal with my frustration, my anger, my sadness, in positive ways. I learned how to harmonize my exuberant feelings, that is, to be emotionally fit. Then, more recently, I learned how to emotionally fit my self to woman, how to open and share my heart in kindness and warmth.

As an adult, I found and developed keen and precise and powerful thoughts. With my imagination and creativeness I constructed my visions in the world and demonstrated my mental fitness. Then, more recently, I discovered the humility of thoughtful service to others and how to mentally fit my self to the needs of community.

As a man I first learned of my capability to capture and hold to my self what was out there in the world. As I grew older I learned how to give back to life by planting seeds and how to use the physical power I have to gift life rather than to take it. As a man, I learned the strength and stamina of my heart, and as I grew older I learned not only to be bold but also to use my feelings to support the disheartened and faltering. As a man, I learned how to brandish the sharp and bright weapons of my mind. But as I grew older, I found that the light of my thoughts might provide a clarity of vision and view much deeper into matters of concern to my family and community. These ways I learned from my relationships with others—from grandparents, parents, spouse, children, and friends—when I was open to enough to their gentle caring and consideration to receive what God was providing through them.

Risking openness

Carolyn: For contacts to strengthen, we have to find within ourselves the ability to trust, not only other people but also God's power that heals us when we are hurt. The healing grows within us the power to connect with others. Until we learn to trust that God does bring new beginnings from dead endings, we will be reluctant and fearful about any kind of suffering, small death, or mortal death. Staying open requires the courage to take whatever comes. The message of the cross tells us that the price of love is often suffering, that death always comes before new life. If what we learn from our life experiences, however, is "duck and hide" rather than "wounds heal," our emotional and spiritual maturity will be stunted.

Spiritual receptivity and emotional openness to other people are closely linked. We cannot receive blessings from our relationships unless we have learned how to be fully present to others. Coming into the presence of God requires that we know what it means to bring our whole selves—heart, mind, and body—into focus. Coming into the presence of God regularly means we have recognized that this is something we long for and need, and make time for. When this happens regularly, a bond, or connection grows. It is a cord of love, to quote the prophet Hosea, that will hold us forever (11:4).

Damian: We cannot be open to relationships with others if we are too full of ourselves, our thoughts, and emotions. If we have too much unregulated energy, we will be frustrated and impatient rather than gentle. We will be angry rather than kind. We will be disgusted with the differences we find in others rather than respectful. Our contacts with others and with God will be difficult at best, painful at worst.

If we bring too little energy into our contacts with others, we will be disappointed and discouraged rather than gentle or patient. We will be fearful rather than generous, and our shame and anguish will prevent us from being able to respect others. Our contacts with others will continue to deplete us.

Learning to still the body and to open ourselves to learning new things will allow us to value and appreciate those we share our lives with. By calming our hearts, we can then mend and tend to the fabric of caring for one another. Knowing how to quiet our mental confusion and distraction can help us perceive and trust the best qualities of others. We can learn to pause and look where God points and to look at others through God's eyes, rather than through the lenses of our own hurt and fear. Then we can see and appreciate the Spirit of God at work in others and in ourselves.

If we are to remain open to others, we must learn to empty ourselves of those things that are not from God. God doesn't send us injury and hurt, coldness and absence. God doesn't send us fear. It takes preparation and maturity to filter out injury and hurt so that we don't pass it on to others. It takes preparation and courage not to disconnect and withdraw from others when we are afraid of pain or injury. It takes reflecting on our past experiences to recognize the habits we may have of withdrawing or withholding kindness from others.

Carolyn: Learning to trust that God has the ability to sustain and heal us allows us to remain open to relationships even when they hurt. Trusting that pain is bearable with the help of God allows us to open our hearts to what others would give even though it may come mixed in with pain. We must learn to sift the "bad apples" from the fruits of the Spirit of God. Trusting that what others intend for evil, as Joseph said, God can use for good, can give us the ability to stay open and connected to others, even when our instincts would prompt us to withdraw.

Perhaps a way to talk about this is with a concrete example. If every negative remark made in my parish about my ministry pierced my heart, I couldn't survive very long as a pastor. However, if I deflect every criticism out of hand, then I am not open to the correction that might be helpful. So I must weigh and sift what comes my way: The hurt, that although pointed at me, has nothing really to do with me I can let go by. The anger that although may sound deeply personal is really fear and projection and has little to do with me. If I am not afraid to stand in the presence of the negative emotions of others, and can deflect the comments while still respecting the speaker, I am learning that I can regulate my own response and with God's help stand my ground without fearing that I don't have the strength or power to withstand attack. It's foolish not to remove yourself from out of control behavior, on the other hand. Where do we draw the line when we are called to "take up our cross"? It is a tricky call. My sense of things is that we have become so fearful these days of the possibility of pain that we risk very few genuine relationships. We have become so protective of our boundaries that we barely let our loved ones close.

If you are to trust God, it's important to learn to pray regularly and listen for God's guidance, or how to come into contact with God. But a chance meeting here and there isn't yet a relationship. It's important to be able to look back through your life and see how faithful and present God has really been. When we begin to see consistent care, that history itself builds confidence and trust. When we can't look over our own stories and see God's consistent way of "showing up" in the past, we have little personal experience that lets us trust God in the future. Learning how to still, calm, and quiet ourselves so that we can recognize when God is present is the first step. Looking back over our lives to see how God has cared for us over time, whether we recognized it or not, is the beginning of telling our faith story. It is the process of connecting individual experiences into a trustworthy thread that has run throughout life.

We have no reason to doubt God's intentions for us, but we have plenty of skepticism to doubt God's presence. Does it say anywhere in Scripture that God has withdrawn from the earth? On the contrary, the God of history promises to be the beginning and end of all life. "As it was in the beginning, is now and ever shall be" might be a guiding principle. Discernment about God's leading and presence is best done within a community of believers. God often comes to us through other people motivated by God to love and serve others. Those who are mature in faith can help us. Without connection to others who are connected to God, we would be left dangling between doubt, uncertainty, and faith.

For personal reflection

Carolyn: Recognizing the gifts God has given to you through relationships is an important step toward recognizing God in your present experience. What were the blessings of your early experiences of love?

Who are the people who have loved you well and pointed you toward God? Who has given you a hand when you felt lost? Who were the angels who ministered to you in times of need? How has God given you the power to heal from times of disconnection and brought you back into connection, with others or with God? Even if people have hurt you, can you see in your story, like Joseph could, that God has been able to work that evil for good? Or do you have wounds that have not healed properly that need attending to? Are you able to see the footprints of God in your story? Do you feel connected or disconnected from God? Do you feel connected or disconnected from other people? Are you too full of yourself or too anxiously self-protective to rely and trust in your most significant relationships? Where does your strength lie, within yourself or with God? Attending honestly to these questions is necessary before anything else is possible.

Spend some quiet time now looking for your patterns and habits.

Relational habits

1. What are your habits of connection with other people?
    - List some of the important people you have had significant relationships with in the past, and what the gifts were in these relationships. Use extra paper or a journal if you need it.
2. What are your habits of disconnection in relationships?
    - When significant relationships have ended, what were the causes? What was your response? How were the hurts healed, if they were? Have these now been forgiven or healed?
3. How has healing and new relational life happened for you?
    - What are your habits of forgiveness in current relationships or in the past? How do conflicts and differences get resolved? What part do you play in these resolutions? What part have others played?

Personal habits

Next identify your patterns of physical, emotional, and mental energy.

Physical energy

1. Stilling the body: What do you do to take care of your body? Do you work out or exercise regularly?
2. Calming the heart: How do you express or let go of feelings?
3. Quieting the mind: Do you meditate or keep a journal? How do you let go of or focus your thoughts?

Emotional energy

1. Connecting with care and empathy: What do you do with negative emotions (anger, fear, frustration)?
2. Positive emotional interchanges: How do you insure support for and from your partner(s)?
3. Uniting cooperatively: How do you deal with conflict between co-workers, supervisors, and family members?

Mental energy

1. Clarifying habitual mental reactions to certain situations and people. How do you verbally and nonverbally communicate your identity as a person, spouse, parent, employee, or community member?
2. Coping with habitual negative thinking or inappropriate reactions to the signals of others. Can you think before you react? Do you know where your reactions come from? What are the signals?
3. Contribution and commitments. Can you work positively within groups until consensus is reached?

Your habits with God

Carolyn: Just like any good parent, God is interested in our growth and well-being. But our individual formation is not all that needs to grow. We also need to grow in our ability to relate to others. All parents hope not only for physically healthy children, but also the progressive abilities to be caring and compassionate, and eventually to make wise decisions! One of my greatest distresses is watching any form of meanness in one of my family members. One of my greatest joys is watching them reach out compassionately. We teach young children not to sit on the kitty, and to care if the food dish is empty. This is relational training.

Damian: Emotional well-being in relationships takes these skills. What are your habits?

- *Caring:* Are you able to listen to others attentively and with empathy?
- *Connecting:* Are you able to appreciate and care for the goodness in others?
- *Communicating:* Are you able to acknowledge and express your understanding of others in positive ways?

Now take some time and think over how these habits with other people impact your habits with God.

- Are you able to let God help you regulate your physical, emotional, and mental energy? Can you make time for God, be open with God and learn new things about God and from God?
- Are you able to let God help you with forgiveness and appreciation in your other relationships and/or in your relationship with God?
- Are you able to see yourself through God's eyes and incorporate that image into your daily living?
- Are you or do you take emotional risks based on your trust in God?

Your faith story

Carolyn: Does your own faith story, your journey or relationship with God, have times of connection, disconnection, and reconnecting? Think about how these things occurred and what role God might have played in them. This story is your faith story, so far in your life.

The next chapter looks at the things that might go wrong or need healing so that your journey can continue in healthy and positive ways.

For group reflection

Share whatever you are comfortable sharing with one other person. Then rejoin the larger group and tell others as much of your story as you are comfortable sharing.

Listen attentively and give each other help in locating the activity of God in your stories. Sometimes, for example, people think that when bad things happened they have been abandoned by God. In those times, if you have that experience, who were the people that showed up with a kind word, a hot meal, or a shoulder? How did healing come from the pain, if it did? What voice inside you gave you strength when you thought you might not survive?

A friend who is a spiritual director told me a story about helping someone find God in her experience of early childhood abuse. My friend asked the woman to remember the painful scene as clearly as she could and look for some evidence of God. Finally she said, "There were many voices. There was the voice that said I must be bad, or God must be doing this to me. But then there was another voice that was very sad and said 'I don't deserve this and somehow I will live through it.' That was God's voice. It was like a quiet friend standing in the corner crying with me."

This, of course, is an extreme example. When I look through my life I have so many stories of the right words of comfort at the right time, the right phone call, the needed assurance, even the strangers who stepped forward and pointed me toward hope and healing. The opportunities that opened up when all I could see was the closing door, I also accept as gifts from God. I was not delivered from suffering, but certainly God never abandoned me in the midst of it. Recognizing this consistency has given me a transformed view of my past and very little fear of the future.

Listen for the good in each other's stories. Sift out the things that are not from God or not intended for "good." Remember that there are other powers at work in the world and in us. We often suffer the consequences of our poor choices. We often suffer at the hands of others who intend us harm. These things aren't from God. But look for the paths that led away from these things toward healing. Who played instrumental parts in those stories? How might they have been vehicles of God's love?

8

Overcoming Obstacles to Connection

Disconnect
Thinking you all alone, I received your gifts
*   and loved you for them.*
Believing that I could give all that was needed in return,
*   I didn't look for God's provision.*
I didn't see the footsteps of God when you walked into my life.
Believing you whole, I railed against your imperfections.
I didn't give you the freedom to be a work in progress,
* like me.*
Believing you whole and alone, I didn't see the hand of God
*   shaping your life, as well as mine.*
I blamed you for your incompleteness,
*   but wanted you to accept mine.*

And only when I had driven you off,
*   did I see where you had truly come from.*
Then I blamed God for taking you away.
Broken open, I was finally prepared
* to meet you for the first time.*
But you had moved on . . . .

*   ⇒ Carolyn*

Carolyn: God gave us life, provision, and also a set of expectations or a guide for what it looks like to love God, our neighbors, and ourselves. I like to think that after God tried many things to help the people of Israel be faithful children, God finally gave them (and us) a very specific list. The Ten Commandments are a pretty clear set of expectations given from a holy parent who loves all the children of creation. God's expectations describe for us how God understands love. They make it possible for us to contribute to the relationship. Even small children who pick dandelions and hand them over proudly are learning how they can make contributions, how they can show love.

Few things are more difficult for me than maintaining one-sided relationships. It feels humiliating to be only on the receiving end. But, there are times in all of our lives when all we can do is receive. Babies, for instance, are completely dependent on the care of others for survival. Very young children soon start looking for ways to be less dependent and to give back. My youngest daughter couldn't pronounce the letter "s" when she was about two. We were continually amused and amazed by how often she stamped her foot on the floor and said "My 'elf!"

But those who are excessively independent, not knowing how to receive or appreciate the gifts others have to give, eventually drive people away. Human relationships can't thrive and grow without learning the skills of "interdependence." For a full relationship, both parties need to make valuable and appreciated contributions. God knows that and takes the dandelions we offer with much more solemnity than they perhaps deserve. That's how it is with love.

God invites us to know his heart: "Be still and know that I am God!" (Psalm 46:10).

In the stillness listen for God and feel God's love: For God, who neither slumbers nor sleeps, watches over Israel and watches over you (Psalm 121:4).

I can't remember a time when I didn't sense God's nearness. From my earliest memories, I can draw from times of charged and moving experiences of God's contact. Unfortunately it doesn't necessarily follow that I've been able to connect the dots and make sense of the picture. The clutter of my other life experiences has often buried God's greatest contributions under piles of dirty laundry and other agendas. Generally I've understood more about what God is, however, than what I am. The surprising thing about pausing, stilling, calming, and quieting is that although I expected to have a deeper experience of God, what I wasn't prepared for was coming into a much greater sense of myself, as discovered through God's presence.

When the heart cries out

Carolyn: Up to this point in the book, we have described a process: beneficial contact that leads to a connection or a bond between two, and in that relationship receiving the gifts that grow our souls. All of this together leads to a full experience of "presence." Being in the presence of God changes our presence and the way we experience life. Others experience the presence of God through encountering us. I think that's what it means to be created in the image of God.

Being in the presence of God, however, also brings us to our knees and often breaks our hearts. We know that the God who can see through our pretenses, posturings, and self-defenses knows the true state of our hearts. We know that we often fall short of being mature and loving people who bring the presence of God to others. We confess that we are broken and often feel God's absence more than God's presence, because our lives are so full of distractions and shadows that disconnect us from God and from each other. We find that when we compare the list of God's expectations and guidance with our responses, that we often fall short—we are more broken than whole. It's then that the gift of God's guidance feels like an impossible demand. We don't experience our civil laws to be a burden until we are no longer keeping them. Rather we see them as necessary for civil peace and well-ordered communities. It's the same with God's Law, or the Ten Commandments. They are a gift and only feel like a burden when we find ourselves straining against them.

God's gifts were intended to help the children of Israel grow and live well. When they rested in their relationship with God and were obedient to God's way of ordering their life, things went well for a time. Human beings, however, experience God's limits as something to push and rail against, rather than as security to rest in. When that happens, we separate ourselves from the love that grows our souls toward mature relationships with God and with each other.

Growth doesn't begin until we have learned to honestly reflect on how we deal with ourselves, the land, the other life around us, and with God's law. To encounter Christ in any meaningful way, we must admit how often we wander in the wilderness, feeling exiled from our true home. To be found requires a pretty clear experience of being lost, kicked out of the garden with only our meager efforts at covering the failures and shortcomings of our lives.

Coming into the presence of God often brings an excruciating sense of where we have been deaf, dumb, and blind to God's love. When the heart cries out for forgiveness, we become at last the good soil, at last prepared for the Word, the good news of Christ. I am a Christian for this reason, rather than a Unitarian: Contact with God often breaks my heart. It drives me to the need for Christ.

Damian: Contact, when it comes, is disturbing and yet we seek more contact. Contact becomes even more inviting as we discover what has been provided, and yet it also becomes more disturbing and painful as we "fall out" of contact.

If only we had a compass and a companion. One to read the map, help us along at each turn, and offer a hand at the inopportune moments when we falter. The peace that is provided is a piece of heaven, not a piece of cake. Mostly we suffer in the "will-derness" and only stumble across the road rather randomly. To stay humbled, not only in the moment of contact-connection-contribution, but also to stay humbled with hope in the suffering, is to kneel and pray for the presence of the Companion, the Compass, and the Guide who saves us from our lonely journeying.

The counterpoint to finding peace in the presence of God is to find the path in the seeming absence of God. That path is the presence of the ever-present Compass and Companion. We find our need for Christ.

Carolyn: When "the first cry of the heart," to use Jean Vanier's language again, has been satisfied—that is, to be held by a mother or father—only then have we been loved well enough to search out an intimate friend, and one to give our hearts to. We cannot respond to Jesus' invitation to follow him when we are looking back over our shoulders needing to love, to forgive, or to bury our dead (Matthew 8:22). We will not be prepared emotionally and spiritually for the life to which Jesus calls us until we have been well loved, comforted, guided, and grown by our heavenly Parent.

If we have never risked connection, there's no need for forgiveness. If we have never experienced pain, there's no need for healing. If we haven't experienced the ache of "disconnection," there's no need for a partner. Until we sense our brokenness, there's no need to be fixed, and no ache for a savior. St. Paul said in his letter to the Galatians "The law was our disciplinarian until Christ came" (3:24).

Go gently now with yourself as you explore what gets in the way of your relationship with God. Most likely it is habits you have developed in your relationships with the people in your life. Name and claim, assess and invite God in. If you are willing to let the old pass away, behold Christ will make all things new!

For Personal Reflection

Carolyn: When I help couples prepare for marriage we use a personal and relationship assessment tool called *Prepare*. It assesses, among other things, the difference in the couple's relational histories from their family of origin. It measures what's normal in one partner and compares it to what's normal for the other partner. Basically it helps the couple look at their habits. Unless they have made a conscious effort to change them, chances are their own idea of marriage will be a replica of what they have experienced or an over-reaction to what they have experienced.

Take some time now to think about your habits. You'll need time, paper, and focus to do this well.

Physically

How close is "close"? How often did your family members stop and spend time with each other? How much connection was normal for you? Did family members play together, work together, eat together, and seek each other out, or did they spend most of their time in separate activities? Has this pattern continued in your adult relationships with your family or siblings? How much time do you now spend in contact with people you care about in order to enjoy them, receive from them, and maintain your connection with them?

Move from your closest circle of immediate family out to your friends and your work relationships. How much time are you physically present in contact with others at your own initiative for the purpose of relationships? When you are physically present with them are you also emotionally and mentally present? How do you know this?

You might ask yourself if you were listening carefully, attending graciously, and giving them your full attention or if you were preoccupied with your own thoughts and feelings.

Emotionally

How emotionally literate, communicative, and available were your parents? How did they express their feelings? How able were they to navigate in negatively charged emotional situations? What did you learn about communicating feelings? How well did you learn to regulate your own emotions? Were your parents able to express care and consideration, kindness and compassion? Were they able to help you soothe the childhood hurts we all experience? When you needed to be held did they hold you? What habits of comfort did they demonstrate? What habits did you learn about negative feelings—anger, hurt, frustration, anxiety? Was it safe to be emotionally close to your parents or did you learn habits of withdrawal and self-protection?

Move from your closest circle of relationships out to your friends and your work or community relationships. How much time do you spend attending to their needs and appreciating their gifts? How do you communicate in these situations? How able are you to regulate your own emotions and help soothe and comfort others? Is the pattern similar to or different from what you learned as a child?

Mentally

What is your interior mental life like? When you are thinking about yourself or others are your thoughts mostly negative or mostly positive? Do you find that you are too easily critical of yourself and others or unable to be honestly critical when you need to be? Think about the conversation patterns demonstrated in your home when you were growing up. Was conversation a means for connecting with each other and strengthening the bonds or a means for "verbal fencing" and establishing superiority, power, or withdrawal? How were differences of opinions handled? Were you allowed to express disagreement? Did you learn to listen and consider the thoughts of others? Or did you fight to be heard, interrupting constantly, seldom attending to the thoughts of others and therefore learning poor listening skills?

Let me give you some examples of conversational habits that are designed to keep distance rather than establish a connection. I can imagine two people sitting on an old-fashioned front porch in a rocking chair. Grandma desires to feel united with grandpa, so through conversation she seeks common ground. She wants her rocker and his rocker to move together on the porch, creating a creaky harmony of togetherness. Grandpa prefers to keep his emotional distance. When grandma rocks forward he rocks backward. When she rocks backwards he pauses and rocks forward. He resists any attempt to find common ground. This is his way of withdrawing from intimacy.

This distancing may happen verbally in several ways. He will disagree with most of her statements, setting up instant discord. He will correct her before she is finished speaking, setting up instant disapproval or a need to be superior. He will remain silent when she tries to engage him, withdrawing altogether. He will "teach" her by offering criticism or unsolicited advice—also a "one-up" move. He will read the paper while she talks to him, signaling that he really doesn't want to attend to what she has to say. He will be quick to be oppositional and slow to come to agreement. He will remove himself from the porch if she doesn't get the message and leave him alone. All of these are methods of withdrawal or protective distance. They are the opposite of caring.

There is one way, however, a grumpy grandpa (or pouting parent, or crabby child—this is an intergenerational pasttime!) might allow verbal agreement. That's in a game called "Ain't It Awful," which was described in a book I read many years ago called *Games People Play*. In this game, conversational pasttiming—the way people communicate in those front-porch-like chats or dinnertime attempts at conversation—is based on finding common negative ground. One person complains about one thing and they both agree that it's "awful." The second person is allowed to bring up another complaint and they both agree that it's "awful." Someone who has a long list of grievances might hit a "home run," as long as they aren't directed at the partner. Consensus is found based on uniting in fear, frustration, impatience, or criticism. For a person seeking connection some consensus may seem better than nothing, but the overall effect is neither pleasant nor mutually building up the body of Christ. It doesn't focus on the good, true, noble, and worthy as St. Paul urges us to do. Grandma may agree to play but in the end it isn't a helpful mental or relational exercise.

We may have learned many habits like this in childhood. One of my adolescent daughter's more comic ways of being grumpy is to plop down on the sofa and invite an argument with a statement like, "I hate our house." At least she's trying to connect, even if it's only to start an argument! We can learn to focus on the good or focus on the bad. We can learn to relate to others primarily to get to gain approval from them or to learn how they might help us. We can compete with others or we can serve them. We can bless or curse them, consciously or in an unconscious repetition of poor relational habits.

Damian: Each of us brings to our relationships physical practices, habits, and conditions within ourselves, some of which are conducive to making our best contributions and some of which undermine our efforts.

Each of us also brings both good and problematic emotional aspects of past and current relationships into our efforts at intimacy with others.

And there are *mental* and social helps and hindrances, supports and difficulties, among us that either contribute to or impede functioning well.

Another way of saying this is that sometimes we have tendencies to withhold or misuse our gifts; sometimes we have tendencies to withdraw from or reject others; and sometimes we obstruct or detract from the efforts of others.

Exercise

Take as much time as you need to reflect on and name your personal habits that seem to be obstacles to connecting.

What needs tending to:

Physically _____

_____

Emotionally _____

_____

Mentally _____

_____

Finally, think about how these habits affect your relationship with God.

1. Are you able to, and do you, physically place yourself and care for yourself in ways that make it possible to grow in relationship to God? If not, how will you change this?

2. Are you emotionally able to let God love you and be empty and calm enough to receive that love? If not, how will you change this?

3. Are you mentally able to listen for God, consider God, and learn new things about God, and then incorporate all of your experience into your daily habits with others? If not, how will you change this?

4. In the days and weeks ahead, how might you begin to learn new habits or practices?

5. How will you also love your neighbors the way you are trying to love God? Or receive from your neighbors the way you are trying to receive from God?

6. Most important, what people will support you in these efforts? Name them here in writing for yourself. Then talk to them about how they can help you—for example, prayer, listening, sharing their observations about you.

For group reflection

Share with one other person some of your thoughts in this section.

Share with the group your hopes for change in the coming weeks and ask for and give prayer support for these efforts.

May our stories help open your hearts to receive the love of God more fully. May you be deeply blessed and be a blessing to those you share your life with. May they be many!

Bibliography

Dunham, Maxie. 1998. *The Workbook of Living Prayer*. Nashville: The Upper Room.

Flanigan, Beverly. 1992. *Forgiving the Unforgivable*. New York: Collier Books.

Foss, Michael. 2000. *Power Surge: Six Marks of Discipleship for a Changing Church*. Minneapolis: Augsburg Fortress.

Foss, Michael. 2002. *A Servant's Manual*. Minneapolis: Fortress Press.

Goleman, Daniel. 1997. *Emotional Intelligence: Why It Can Matter More Than IQ*. New York: Bantam Books.

Gottman, John and Nan Silver. 1999. *Seven Principles for Making Marriage Work*. New York: Three Rivers Press.

Hanson, Bradley. 1990. *Teach Us to Pray: Overcoming Obstacles to Prayer*. Minneapolis: Augsburg Fortress.

Kallestad, Walt. 1995. *The Everyday, Anytime Guide to Prayer*. Minneapolis: Augsburg Fortress Books.

Nesser, Joann. 1998. *Journey into Reality: Through Prayer and God-Centeredness*. Prior Lake, Minn: Living Waters Publishing.

Poling-Goldenne, David and Shannon Jung. 2001. *Discovering Hope: Building Vitality in Rural Congregations*. Minneapolis: Augsburg Fortress.

Richo, David. 1997. *When Love Meets Fear: How to Become Defense-less and Resource-full*. Mahwah, New Jersey: Paulist Press.

Strobel, Lee. 2000. *The Case for Faith: A Journalist Investigates the Toughest Objections to Christianity*. Grand Rapids, Mich.: Zondervan.

Vraniak, Damian. 2003. *Healing the Helper: Therapy for Professionals*. Madison, Wis: Women's Education Network.

Vraniak, Damian and David McKee.1995. *Parssiterns: The Parts, Processes, Principles and Patterns of Transformation, Vol. I (of IV)*. Madison, Wis.: White Wolf.

Vraniak, Damian and William Schmelzer. 2002. *Successful Parenting*. Hayward, Wis.: Advanced Printing Press.

Yancey, Philip. 2001. *Reaching for the Invisible God*. Grand Rapids, Mich.: Zondervan.